Welcome to *Explodapedia*, the indispensable guide to everything you need to know!
This series is packed with in-depth knowledge you can trust; it gives you the tools you need to understand the science behind the wonders of our world. *The Gene* is a vital chapter of our story, so read on to discover what makes you, you . . .

'Extraordinary discoveries are explained in a way everyone can understand.'
Sir Paul Nurse, Nobel Prize winner

'The perfect balance between charm, quirkiness and wonder . . . for kids and adults alike.'
Siddhartha Mukherjee, Pulitzer Prize winner

'A totally fascinating book, brimming with amazing scientific knowledge and fab illustrations.' **Greg Jenner**

'Successfully blend[s] appealingly humorous drawings . . . [with] text that combines clarity and accuracy.'
Professor Richard Fortey

'Both accessible and funny . . . a clever way to introduce . . . our understanding of all life today.'
Professor Venki Ramakrishnan, Nobel Prize winner

BM: To Andy, whose memory, and genes, live on in me;
and now in Beda and Ghyll too.

AA: To Karen, Connor and Spencer – I love what you've done with your genes!

EXPLODAPEDIA
THE GENE
What Makes You, You?

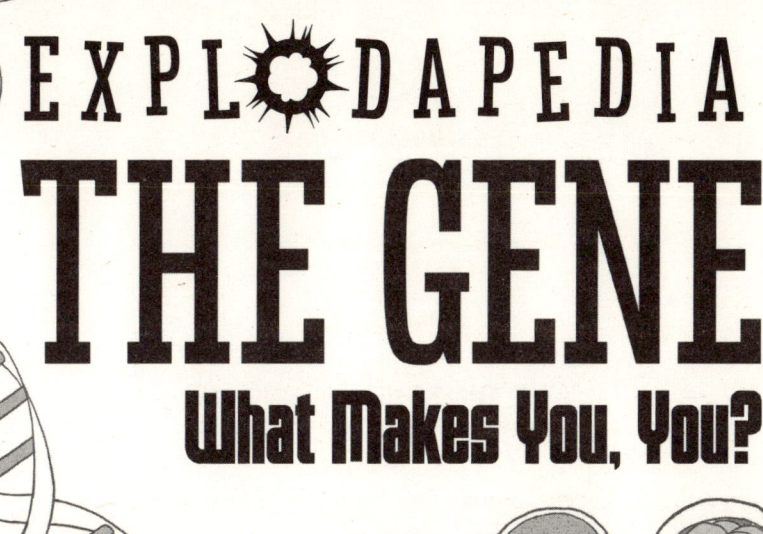

Ben Martynoga

Illustrated by
Moose Allain

David Fickling Books

31 Beaumont Street
Oxford OX1 2NP, UK

Explodapedia: The Gene
is a
DAVID FICKLING BOOK

First published in Great Britain in 2023 by
David Fickling Books,
31 Beaumont Street,
Oxford, OX1 2NP

Text © Ben Martynoga, 2023
Illustrations © Moose Allain, 2023

978-1-78845245-8

1 3 5 7 9 10 8 6 4 2

The right of Ben Martynoga and Moose Allain to be identified as the author and illustrator of this work has been asserted in accordance with the Copyright, Designs and Patents Act 1988.

All rights reserved. No part of this publication may be reproduced, stored in a retrieval system, or transmitted in any form or by any means, electronic, mechanical, photocopying, recording or otherwise, without the prior permission of the publishers.

Papers used by David Fickling Books are from well-managed forests and other responsible sources.

DAVID FICKLING BOOKS Reg. No. 8340307

A CIP catalogue record for this book is available from the British Library.

Printed and bound in Great Britain by Clays, Ltd, Elcograf S.p.A.

Italic type is used in *Explodapedia* to highlight words that are defined in the glossary when they first appear, to show quoted material and the names of published works. Bold type is used for emphasis.

Contents

What Makes You, **You**	7
Chapter 1: From Pea Production to Reproduction	14
Chapter 2: So That's What a Gene Looks Like	25
Chapter 3: DNA Takes Charge	41
Chapter 4: Cooking Up a Human	54
Chapter 5: Meet Your Genome	67
Chapter 6: Mutant Invasion	77
Chapter 7: The History of You	90
Chapter 8: Sunshine and Showers	102
Chapter 9: DNA is not Destiny	114
Chapter 10: Messing Around with Genes	126
There's No Such Thing as Normal	142
Timeline	148
Glossary	150
Index	155
Acknowledgements	158
About the Author and Illustrator	159

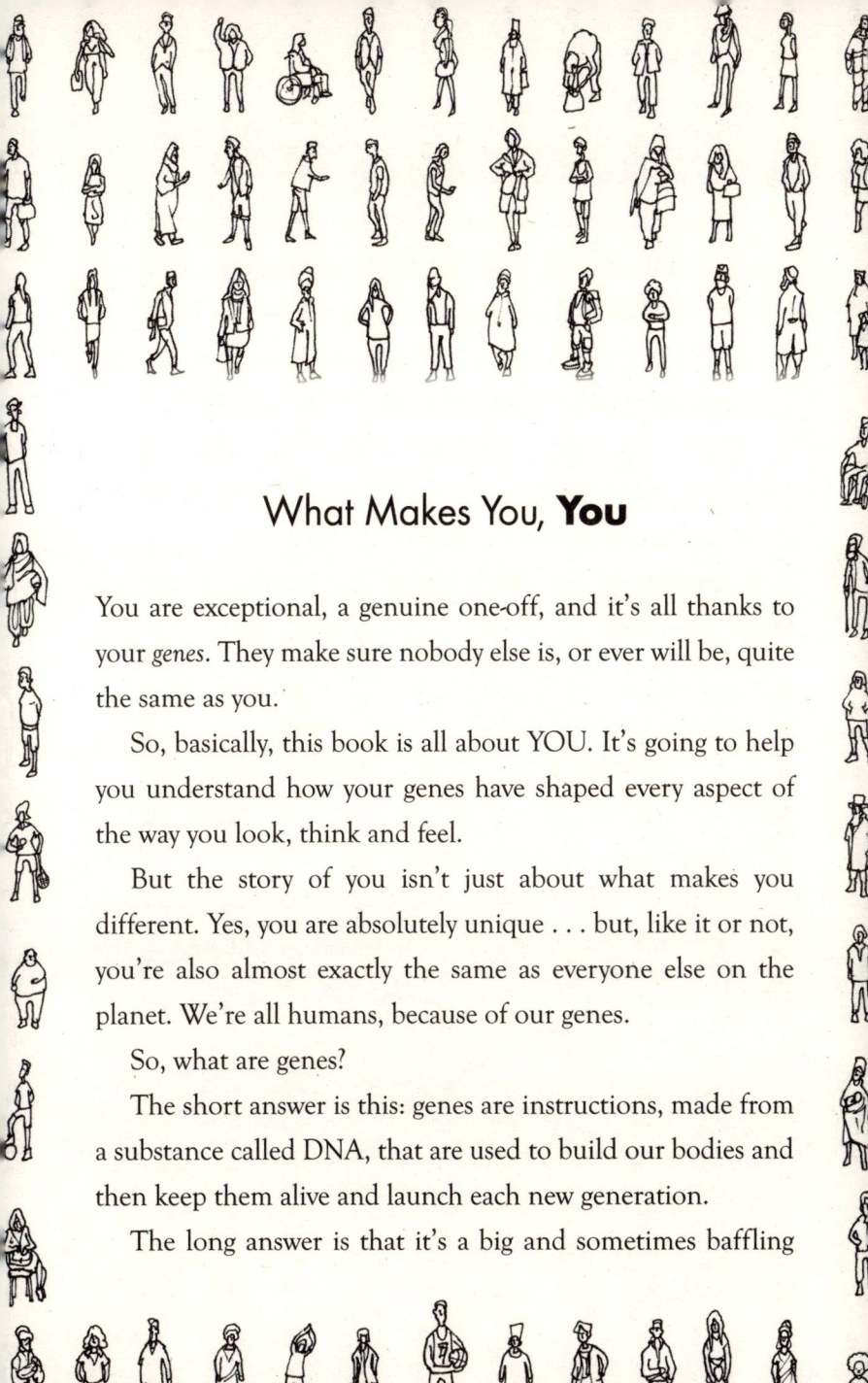

What Makes You, **You**

You are exceptional, a genuine one-off, and it's all thanks to your *genes*. They make sure nobody else is, or ever will be, quite the same as you.

So, basically, this book is all about YOU. It's going to help you understand how your genes have shaped every aspect of the way you look, think and feel.

But the story of you isn't just about what makes you different. Yes, you are absolutely unique . . . but, like it or not, you're also almost exactly the same as everyone else on the planet. We're all humans, because of our genes.

So, what are genes?

The short answer is this: genes are instructions, made from a substance called DNA, that are used to build our bodies and then keep them alive and launch each new generation.

The long answer is that it's a big and sometimes baffling

topic: even expert biologists spend a lot of time arguing about what exactly a gene is. So, we're going to take things one step at a time and gradually build up a clearer picture of the gene. By the end of the book, though, you'll hopefully see how genes do what seems impossible: they make you virtually identical to everyone else AND entirely individual at the same time.

In fact, genes are completely essential for pretty much everything **all** living things do. Without genes there'd be absolutely no life on planet Earth.

Look, here's a gene. Hello there. Can you tell us how you do what you do?

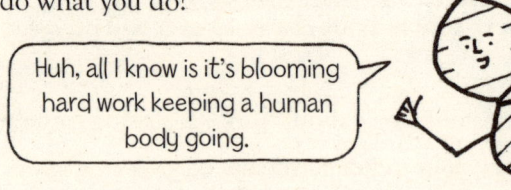

To be fair you're just a long, wriggly molecule of DNA. There's no way you could understand quite how important you are to our lives. You probably shouldn't even be talking to us.

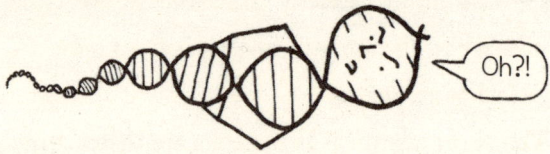

But can you stick around? Maybe you can help us find out more about what genes are and how they work.

Genes were one of the main things that really got life on Earth started in the first place, about four thousand million years ago, and they've been at the very heart of the action ever since. So, believe it or not, some of the genes in your body are practically identical to genes found inside every other creature you'll ever see, from the microscopic *bacteria* growing between your teeth, to the fly buzzing around that banana in your fruit bowl, to the cat that wants to catch the fly, to the banana itself. Because of your genes, you've got a surprising amount in common with all other living things. They're part of your story too.

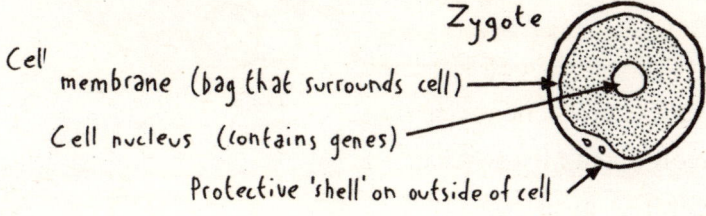

Phew. There's a lot to cover, so let's start telling the story of you from the very beginning.

Does this picture look familiar?

No? Well, it's actually a picture of you when you were younger . . . much younger. You could say it was your first baby snap. You didn't recognize yourself, because your picture is exactly the same as everyone else's at that age.

Let's zoom in a bit:

Scientists call this a *zygote*, and that's all there was to your body in the beginning: a single *cell*, squishy, round and about as tall and wide as a sheet of paper is thick. But today you're not just one cell big, you're formed from trillions of different cells that are all working together to make you. Those cells all look, more or less, like the one on page 9; in fact, all living things are made up of cells that aren't so very different from this one.

The cells in your body all grew from that zygote, which was formed when an egg cell from your biological* mother was *fertilized* by a sperm cell from your biological father. When that happened, a bunch of genes that once belonged to your dad and another set of genes from your mum were mixed together to make a completely new set of genes: **your** genes.

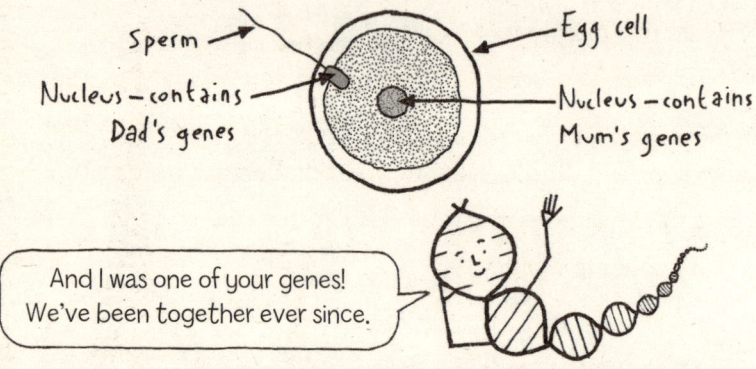

*Your *biological parents* are the ones who provided the egg and sperm you grew from. They may not be the people you call your parents today, but that's who we're referring to in the rest of this section.

That little zygote may have been small and squishy, but, with its shiny new set of genes, it was a thing of wonder.

It contained all the instructions needed to build and then run an entire, fully formed human: YOU!

Gene instructions work like coded messages. They're written in a mysterious alphabet made up of just four different letters. Genes are 'information' in solid chemical form – *genetic information*. Living cells contain a stupendous amount of it.

Even as a single-celled zygote, you contained 6.2 BILLION letters of code

Print all that code in books like this one, and you'd fill 49,000 volumes

Stack those volumes up and they'd be taller than the Eiffel Tower in Paris

Somehow, all that information was packed away inside a minute cell that could be balanced on the sharp end of a pin. And an entire copy of that genetic information – every last letter of it – is tucked away inside almost every cell in your body today.

But what does it say? What secret messages are hidden away inside your genes?

Well, if you tried to read the code from scratch, it would look like utter gobbledegook. But, over the years, biologists have got better and better at making sense of it. They've discovered that genes are actually chock-full of stories – about things that happened long before you were born, things that are happening to you right now, and things that will happen to you in the future.

> We may just be long, wriggly *molecules*, but we know things about you that you don't know about yourself!

And, dear reader, the stories written in your genes aren't there for entertainment, they can have a massive effect on your life. For example, they can:

• Identify close relatives you never knew you had.

• Predict which illnesses you'll suffer from decades from now – maybe even when and how you'll die!

• Predict what your future children might look like, long before they're born.

These days scientists can't just **read** the information stored inside genes. They can also **edit** genes, **erase** them and even **rewrite** them. That means they can make up completely new gene-based stories. So far, they've mainly done this with non-human living things, such as bacteria, food plants and farm animals. Some of these genetic creations could help us to grow food in new ways, or destroy pollution – but it's also possible that some of them could harm humans, or the natural world we live in.

However, now it's even possible to edit and rewrite **human** genes – including your genes.

You're right to be concerned. Genes – and the stories they contain – must be handled with great care. Altering them can have vast and truly life-changing effects, for better or for worse. Scientists still have a huge amount to find out about genes. And we do too. So, if we're going to get to grips with how genes make you, **you** and how they breathe life into the world, we'd better get on with it.

CHAPTER 1
From Pea Production to Reproduction
WHAT ARE GENES FOR?

The biggest problem with life is . . . death. All living things will die, eventually, so if they don't want to go extinct – and frankly, who does? – they simply have to *reproduce*. Most creatures are very good at this; you could say it's what they live for. Trees make seeds, birds hatch chicks, flies lay eggs, mould spreads, *microbes* make more microbes and people have babies. Living things do all this multiplying for themselves – it's known as *reproduction*.

Lots of living things, including bacteria and bread yeast, live their lives as single, independent cells. They might reproduce to spread a nasty infection across your tonsils, or to make bread dough rise. Here's how it happens:

1. Cell follows gene instructions in order to grow bigger.

2. Cell makes complete copy of all its genes.

3. Cell chops itself in half, making absolutely sure that both new cells end up with a full set of genes.

4. One cell has turned itself into two cells.

This is called cell division and it is the most basic and the most common form of reproduction in the living world.

The cells that make up your body reproduce in the same way. They're all little living beings in their own right and they are all created by *cell division*. Whenever part of your body grows or a cut heals, the new cells that are needed get churned out by existing cells that reproduce themselves by cell division.

Lots of plants and fungi, and a smaller number of animals (e.g. starfish and flatworms) use this kind of cell division, called *mitosis*, to make whole new bodies. If some of their cells bud off, or get broken off accidentally, those cells divide, over and over, eventually making an entire new creature.

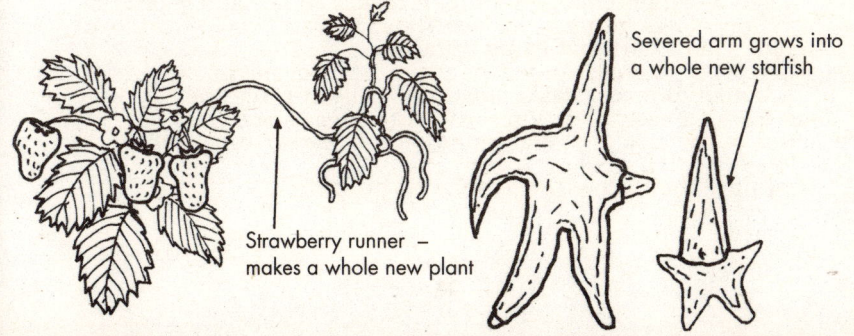

Strawberry runner – makes a whole new plant

Severed arm grows into a whole new starfish

But for animals like us, reproduction is a bit more complicated. As you know, it takes cells from two different people to make a baby: a male sperm and a female egg must fuse themselves – and their genes – together to make a new cell. This is called *sexual reproduction*. Lots of plants do it in a similar way:

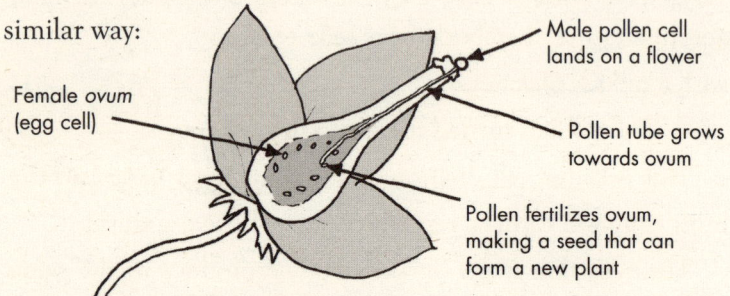

If we skip over the details of how sperm and egg, or pollen and ovum, get mixed together, then the end result of sexual reproduction isn't all that different from the division of single cells.

THE SAME, BUT DIFFERENT

When a computer copies a file, it makes an absolutely perfect copy. That's not what living things do.

Sometimes cells make mistakes while copying their genes. And in the case of sexual reproduction, living things mix and reshuffle their gene instructions on purpose.

It might sound like these errors and intentional mix-ups should cause problems. Sometimes they do – things can go wrong if essential parts of the gene instructions are damaged or destroyed. But overall it's worth the risk, because living things very often need their next generation to be the same, but different.

Eh? Why don't they want them exactly the same?

Well, the world is always changing. If living things can only ever copy their gene instructions perfectly, they can't change themselves. And if they can't change themselves, their old tricks are bound to stop working, sooner or later.

Dinner's up!

Huh, maybe for you, Mrs Longneck!

The living things that have survived the longest are the ones that managed to find the right balance between copying their genes perfectly and changing them, often just a tiny bit, from one generation to the next.

Think about your parents.

In lots of ways they're exactly the same as you. Count your fingernails, eyes, toes, nostrils, belly buttons, limbs and nipples. Chances are the number and overall shape of your body parts are pretty much the same.

But you're also very different from your parents – thank goodness – and not just because they're much older than you.

For starters, if you were born male, some of your body parts will definitely be different from your mum's, and if you were born female, you'll obviously be different from your dad. But there are loads of smaller differences too. You might share the colour of your hair, eyes or skin with just one parent – or neither of them.

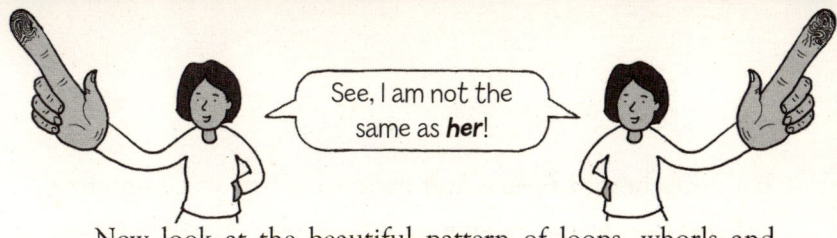

See, I am not the same as *her*!

Now look at the beautiful pattern of loops, whorls and ridges on the tips of your fingers. Nobody else in the universe has the same fingerprints as you – even if you have an identical twin.

All of these *characteristics* are strongly influenced by the genes your parents gave you. But your mum and dad each had their own genes. How did their genes get mixed together to make yours?

To explain it all properly, and find out how genes were discovered, we're going to take a quick trip 160 years back in time, to Silesia. Today, that's a region of the Czech Republic.

Like Genes in a Pod?

We're in a huge greenhouse in the garden of a monastery in the city of Brno, about to meet gardener extraordinaire, Gregor Mendel.

Mendel is also a monk

Ahoj!*

and a highly trained scientist. He's brilliant at maths and particularly loves growing peas, but not to eat them.

We're in the 1860s, so, like everyone else of his day, Mendel

*That's hi in Czech, by the way.

has never heard of genes and only has a hazy understanding of how sexual reproduction actually works. But, weirdly, he thinks his pea plants can fill in the missing blanks.

There are thousands of pea plants in this greenhouse. They're all the same because, well, they're all peas. But they're also different because Mendel has grown lots of varieties of pea that each have unique features. For example, some plants produce green peas, but others produce yellow peas. Mendel tried crossing a yellow pea plant with a green pea plant . . .

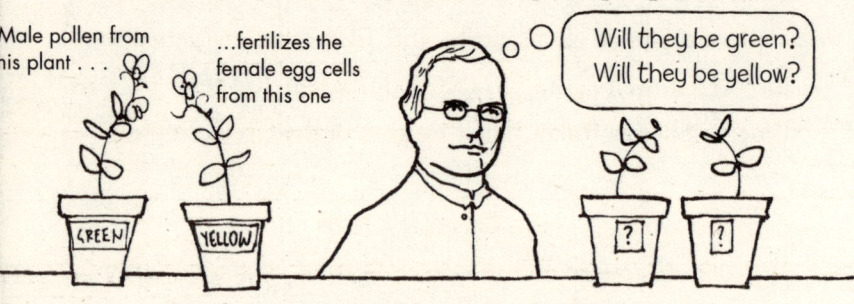

. . . But the next generation astounded him.

Mendel crossed the new yellow pea plants with each other and, in the third generation, green peas were suddenly back in the mix. Whatever turned the peas green had somehow missed a generation and then come back.

With the help of his garden assistants, Mendel started

crossing all sorts of different pea plants with each other. He saw exactly the same pattern every time: with each pair he crossed, one of the features of the parent plants always skipped a generation, then reappeared.

From these results, Mendel made a dazzling leap. He went straight from counting up the different characteristics of the pea plants to working out how something in the plant was passing on instructions from one generation to the next.

Here are Mendel's most important conclusions:

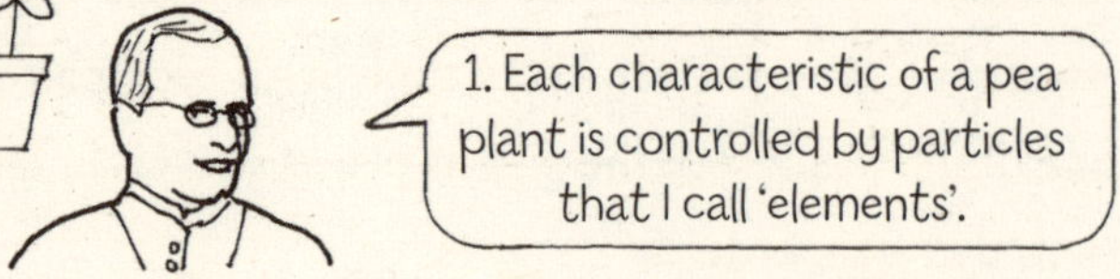

> 1. Each characteristic of a pea plant is controlled by particles that I call 'elements'.

Elements are what we call genes, and Mendel worked out that there must be elements, or genes, that control a plant's seed colour, flower colour, root length, leaf number, height and countless other characteristics.

> 2. Each element exists as a pair.

Yes, as with most *species* that reproduce sexually, there are two copies of each pea gene, one inherited from the male parent and one from the female parent.

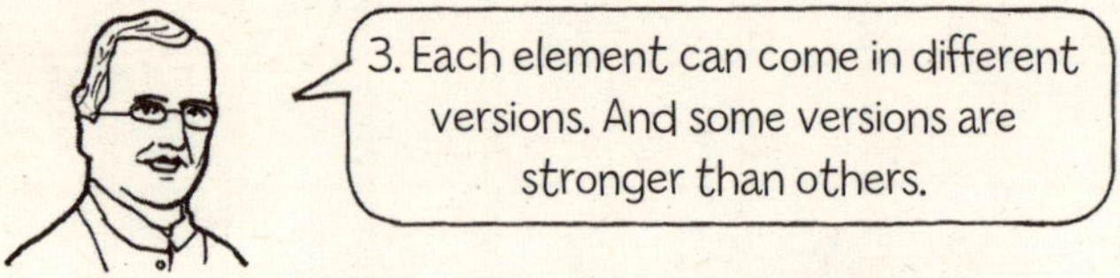

> 3. Each element can come in different versions. And some versions are stronger than others.

In Mendel's first experiment, the pea plants inherited one yellow and one green version of the pea colour gene.

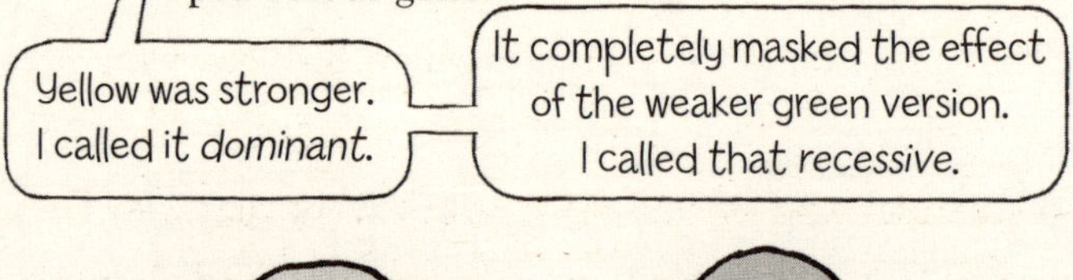

> Yellow was stronger. I called it *dominant*.

> It completely masked the effect of the weaker green version. I called that *recessive*.

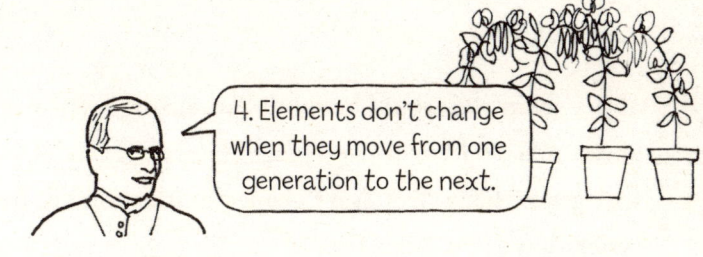

That means recessive versions of a gene don't get altered or disappear – their effects are only hidden by a dominant version, so they can still be passed down to the next generation. That's why the green pea colour was able to miss a generation and then reappear whenever a plant inherited the green, recessive gene from **both** parents.

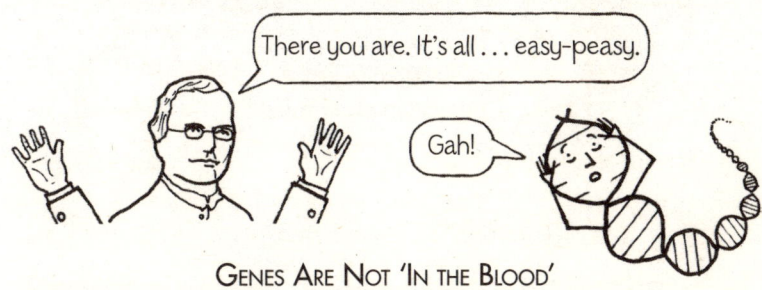

Genes Are Not 'In the Blood'

Before Mendel, nobody had a clue about how inheritance worked. One popular idea was that information about a person's body was somehow carried in their blood. When two people had a baby, the two streams of blood got merged together. People still talk about family characteristics being 'in the blood' today, even though we know that isn't literally true.

It was Mendel who proved things can't work that way. For a start, pea plants don't have any blood! But if inheritance really did involve true blending, then crossing a yellow pea

and a green pea would be more like mixing paint – it would always make yellowish-green peas. Thanks to Mendel, we know that genes themselves don't change much, if at all, from one generation to the next. They're usually there or not there – like the pieces of a jigsaw puzzle.

In the 1860s, Mendel's ideas were totally new and unexpected. Other scientists completely failed to grasp the significance of what he was saying.

Then, in around 1900, by total coincidence, three different biologists stumbled across Mendel's masterpiece in the pages of an obscure scientific journal and realized his ideas were absolutely right.

At long last, people started to recognize Mendel's brilliance. And so began the long process of proving that genes don't just exist in peas; they're the essential operating instructions for all living things, from pond scum to peanuts, pelicans, pandas, people and everything else in between.

CHAPTER 2
So That's What a Gene Looks Like
HUNTING DOWN DNA

Proving that genes must exist answered some big questions. But, like most steps forward in science, it raised many more. Most pressing of all was: what are these mysterious gene things actually made of?

Funnily enough, the first clue to solving that mystery was uncovered in 1869, just a couple of years after Mendel first wrote about his gene idea.

It was a dark winter's evening, and a young scientist called Friedrich Miescher was prowling the wards of his local hospital in the German city of Tübingen.

Pus, as you may or may not wish to know, is the whitish-yellow stuff that builds up in infected cuts and sores. Miescher was a chemist, and he very much wanted to find out what cells are made from. He knew pus mainly consisted of white blood cells that have died while helping the body to fight infection.

Miescher was particularly interested in one specific part of the cell: the *nucleus*. It seemed obvious to him that the nucleus must do something very important. Why else would nearly every animal and plant cell have one?

Once he explained what he was doing, the hospital staff gladly gave him as many dirty bandages as he could ever want. Back in his lab, he did lots of different chemical tests on the cell nuclei and found that they were almost entirely made from just two different substances:

- *Protein*. Miescher was expecting this, because proteins form most of the structures, moving parts and control systems that keep cells alive.

- And a chemical that had never been identified before. It looked like a white cloud of fine, wispy strands. He called the substance *nuclein* because the nucleus was full of it.

Nuclein – now known as DNA

Today, we call 'nuclein' *deoxyribonucleic acid*, or *DNA* for short.

Miescher was staring at millions and millions of human genes, without even realizing what a massive discovery he'd made. But it wasn't until both scientists were dead that anybody linked Miescher's 'nuclein' and Mendel's 'elements'.

Even in the early 1900s, when most scientists had finally accepted that genes do indeed exist, hardly any of them thought genes had anything to do with DNA.

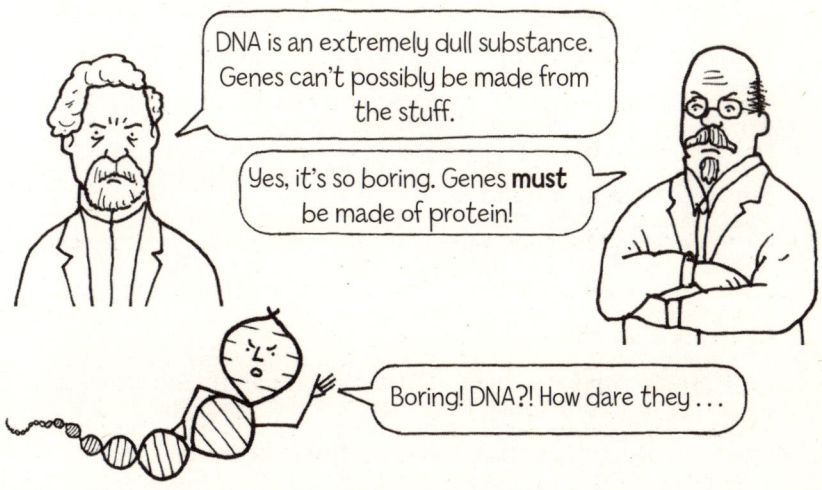

Well, the sceptical scientists had a point. Proteins come in all sorts of weird and wonderful shapes, so it seemed much more likely that they would be the ones that spelled out genetic information. DNA, on the other hand, looked like it was made up of just four different kinds of molecule, which linked together in long chains like this:

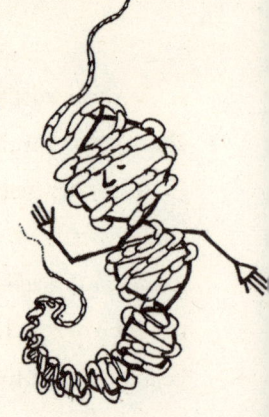

Maybe it wraps itself round genes to protect them?

The possibility that genes **were** DNA barely occurred to any of them.

So, Is DNA Dull?

Finally, in 1944, 75 years after Miescher had first identified it, a Canadian biologist called Oswald Avery decided to start taking DNA seriously. He did an experiment that appeared to show that the genes of bacteria are made of DNA, not protein.

Questioning new findings is an important part of being a scientist, but sometimes it can go too far. And, too bad for Avery, many biologists simply refused to believe him.

Then, in 1952, two scientists, Martha Chase and her boss, Alfred Hershey, managed to turn the tide.

We think *viruses* can tell us what genes are and settle this matter, once and for all.

Viruses can't actually tell us anything, of course – they are the smallest and simplest living forms of all. But they definitely do contain genes and, for Chase and Hershey, that was their power.

Viruses are living things, but they can't reproduce themselves on their own. Instead they use their **virus** genes to force the cells of **other** living things to do all the hard work of making more viruses.

The question was, which part of the virus's little bodies were the genes?

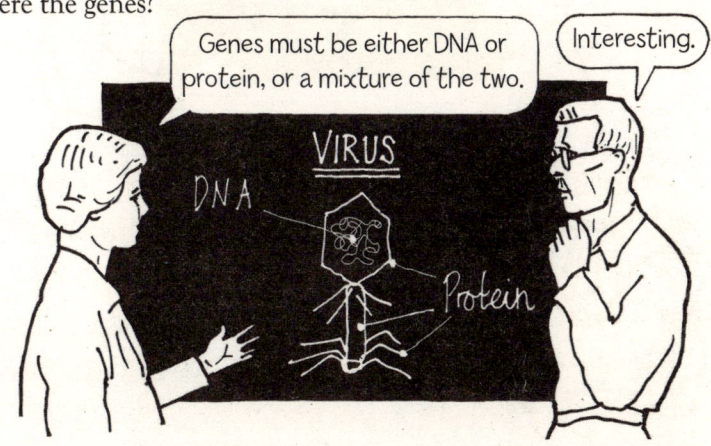

To find out, Chase attached a tiny chemical label to the virus's DNA, and a different chemical label to its protein parts. Then she used the labelled viruses to infect bacteria cells. Whichever virus parts ended up inside infected cells had to be the genes.

Their results were crystal clear. Only the DNA entered the

bacteria cells. And that DNA was definitely powerful stuff. It forced the infected cells to produce so many fully formed new viruses – made up of DNA **and** protein – that the bacteria burst open and died.

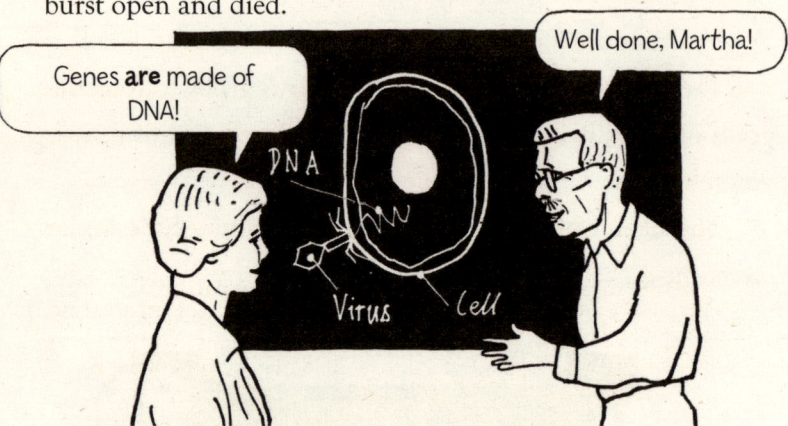

This time, at long last, the world listened, and a few years later, Chase and Hershey's discovery was rewarded with a Nobel Prize – the biggest prize a scientist can get. But it went to the boss, Hershey. Despite her crucial input, Martha didn't even get a mention in his acceptance speech.

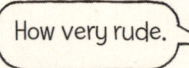

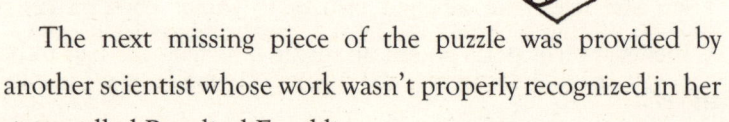

The next missing piece of the puzzle was provided by another scientist whose work wasn't properly recognized in her time, called Rosalind Franklin.

DNA Is Not Dull!

Once all scientists had accepted that genes really were made of DNA, the next burning challenge was to understand how DNA actually carries the information needed to make and run living things.

The best way to do that was to see what DNA molecules actually look like. If scientists could find out how it was built, *atom* by atom, DNA would surely reveal its secrets.

But how? DNA molecules can be very long, but they are almost unimaginably thin. They measure just 2.3 *nanometres* across. If they were lined up side by side, it would take at least 100,000 DNA molecules to cover the width of this letter: l.

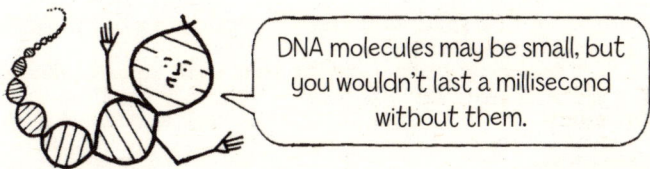

DNA molecules may be small, but you wouldn't last a millisecond without them.

Back in the 1950s, there was no way even the most powerful electron microscopes could make out the details of something so incredibly slender as DNA.

But Rosalind Franklin was a world expert in a technique called *X-ray crystallography*. It relied on the fact that solid, 3D objects, no matter how small they are, all cast shadows.

Ordinary light wouldn't reveal shadows made by molecules like DNA, so Franklin used beams of super-intense X-ray light.

Franklin and her team eventually managed to get crisp photographs of DNA's minuscule shadow. It looked a bit like this:

Exactly. The next task – a tough one – was to use the shapes and angles of that shadow pattern to build up a 3D portrait of the DNA molecule itself. Getting that right would take some complicated mathematical equations and a large dollop of imagination.

Franklin took the crucial pictures and made good progress in analysing them, but at the end of the day, she didn't actually work out how DNA was built. It was Francis Crick and James Watson, two scientists working together at Cambridge University, who solved the puzzle of the century. In 1953, they showed the world exactly how the atoms of DNA fit together.

Nine years later, in 1962, Crick and Watson won a Nobel Prize for their massive achievement. Franklin's colleague,

Maurice Wilkins, shared the prize with them, but Franklin couldn't claim her slice of the glory – she'd died of cancer four years earlier, aged just 37. She had played a vital role in one of the biggest scientific discoveries of all time, though. Crick and Watson couldn't have slotted the pieces together without Franklin's X-ray pictures.

Now, prepare for your mind to be well and truly boggled as we unpick their brilliant breakthrough.

DNA IS A TWIRLY-WHIRLY SELF-COPYING CODE MACHINE

Here's what a DNA molecule looks like up close. You can think of it as working a bit like the zip on your hoodie.

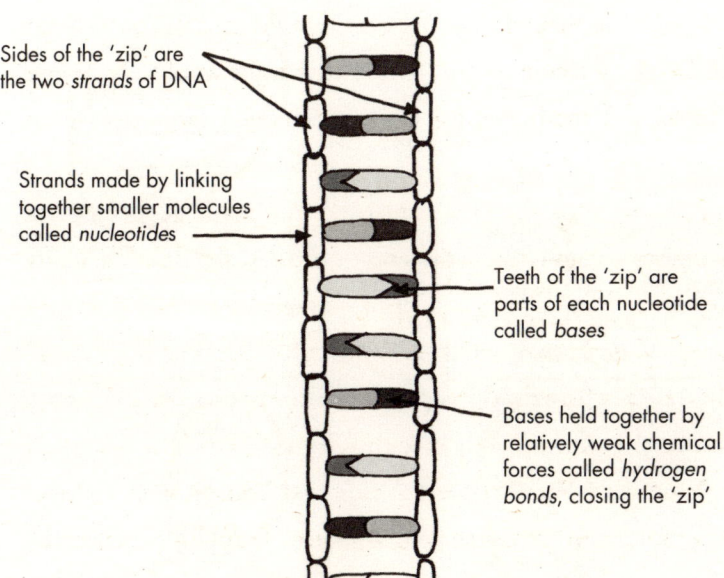

Sides of the 'zip' are the two *strands* of DNA

Strands made by linking together smaller molecules called *nucleotides*

Teeth of the 'zip' are parts of each nucleotide called *bases*

Bases held together by relatively weak chemical forces called *hydrogen bonds*, closing the 'zip'

These molecules can be very long indeed; they're made up of millions or even billions of nucleotides, joined side by side, in each of DNA's two connected strands.

Unlike the zip on your hoodie, the DNA zip is twisted into a spiral called a *double helix*:

Isn't it just? But that's not what Crick and Watson found most amazing about it.

Job 1: Spell Out Life's Information
Here's how. The bases of the nucleotides that make up DNA come in four 'flavours': adenine, thymine, cytosine and guanine. We'll call them A, T, C and G; it's easier to say and they really do act like letters. The sentence you're reading right now uses a 26-letter alphabet, but the DNA alphabet is made up of just four different letters. The letters in DNA messages aren't printed in flat lines that run back and forth across a page, they're spelled out by the order in which the nucleotide letters (A, T, C and G) appear in the DNA double helix.

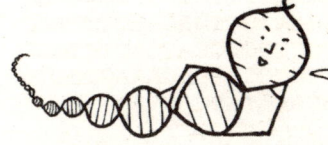

You'll be amazed what we can do with those four letters.

We definitely will. Each gene is a stretch of DNA that spells out a set of instructions for building a particular part of a cell. These parts are often made from protein and they work together to help an *organism* grow, survive and reproduce.

Gene, you're a type of gene that exists inside every human being, so let's use you to show how this works.

Righto.

The instructions you contain tell a cell how to make a particularly important protein molecule that forms part of *haemoglobin*, the substance that carries oxygen around our bodies in our blood. More on this in Chapter 3.

Haemoglobin looks like this:

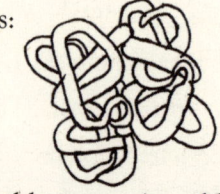

And your instructions to build it are written like this:

```
ATGGTGCATCTGACTCCTGAGGAGAAGTCTGCCGTTACTGCCCTG
TGGGGCAAGGTGAACGTGGATGAAGTTGGTGGTGAGGCCCTGGGC
AGGCTGCTGGTGGTCTACCCTTGGACCCAGAGGTTCTTTGAGTCC
TTTGGGGATCTGTCCACTCCTGATGCTGTTATGGGCAACCCTAAG
GTGAAGGCTCATGGCAAGAAAGTGCTCGGTGCCTTTAGTGATGGC
CTGGCTCACCTGGACAACCTCAAGGGCACCTTTGCCACACTGAGT
GAGCTGCACTGTGACAAGCTGCACGTGGATCCTGAGAACTTCAGG
CTCCTGGGCAACGTGCTGGTCTGTGTGCTGGCCCATCACTTTGGC
AAAGAATTCACCCCACCAGTGCAGGCTGCCTATCAGAAAGTGGTG
GCTGGTGTGGCTAATGCCCTGGCCCACAAGTATCACTAA
```

(We did say DNA was mind-boggling stuff!)

Each human cell contains around 20,000 genes that work in more or less the same way as Gene. They all contain messages that look very much like this one, messages that tell cells how to make a specific working part of themselves. Together, they make us what we are. They keep us alive.

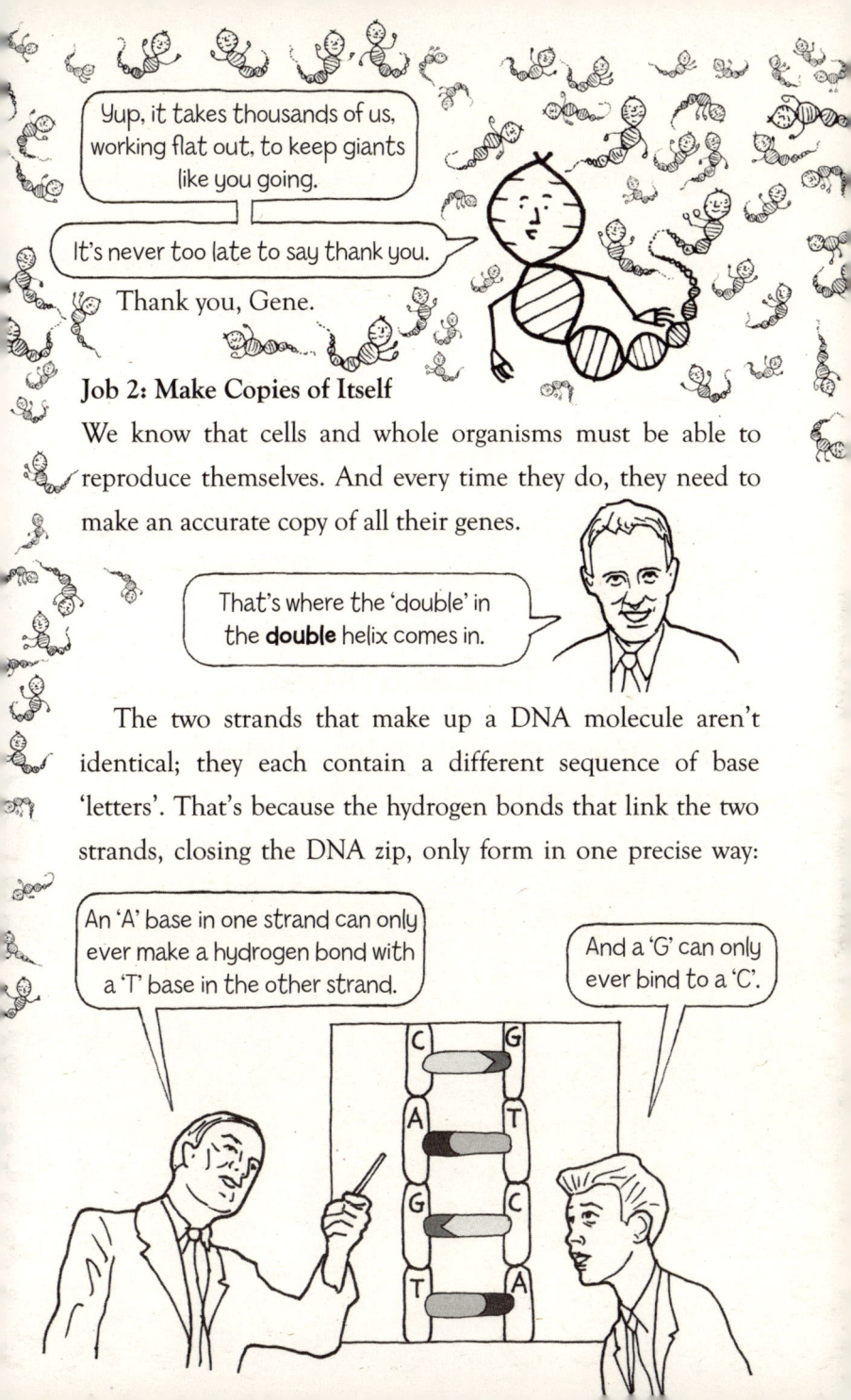

> Yup, it takes thousands of us, working flat out, to keep giants like you going.

> It's never too late to say thank you.

Thank you, Gene.

Job 2: Make Copies of Itself

We know that cells and whole organisms must be able to reproduce themselves. And every time they do, they need to make an accurate copy of all their genes.

> That's where the 'double' in the **double** helix comes in.

The two strands that make up a DNA molecule aren't identical; they each contain a different sequence of base 'letters'. That's because the hydrogen bonds that link the two strands, closing the DNA zip, only form in one precise way:

> An 'A' base in one strand can only ever make a hydrogen bond with a 'T' base in the other strand.

> And a 'G' can only ever bind to a 'C'.

This is called *base pairing*, and every cell on the planet does it in exactly the same way. That means, if you know the order of DNA letters on one strand of DNA, you can be 100% certain of the order of letters on the other strand.

Here's the code for the start of Gene's information-carrying strand again:

ATGGTGCATCTG

By pairing As with Ts and Cs with Gs, we can be sure that the matching strand of the DNA double helix **must** read like this:

TACCACGTAGAC

And if we put both strands together and uncoil that piece of DNA from its helix shape, it looks like this:

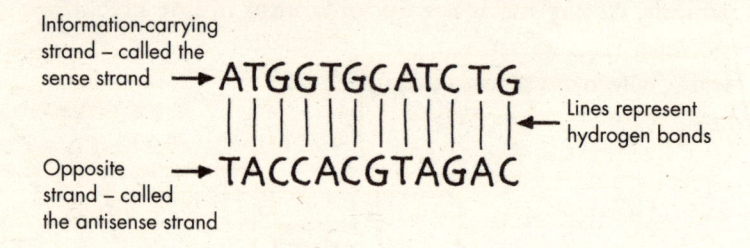

```
Information-carrying
strand – called the
sense strand      → ATGGTGCATCTG
                    ||||||||||||  ← Lines represent
                                    hydrogen bonds
Opposite          → TACCACGTAGAC
strand – called
the antisense strand
```

Because the mirror-image strand can only form in one totally predictable way, cells make perfect copies of their genes **nearly** every time they divide. Here's how:

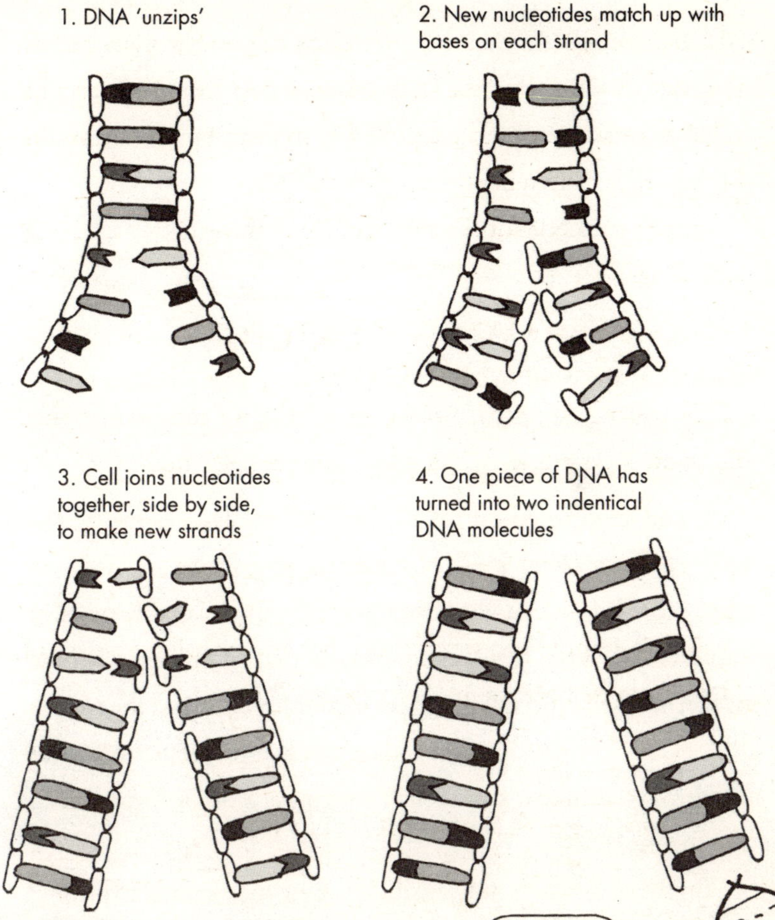

1. DNA 'unzips'

2. New nucleotides match up with bases on each strand

3. Cell joins nucleotides together, side by side, to make new strands

4. One piece of DNA has turned into two indentical DNA molecules

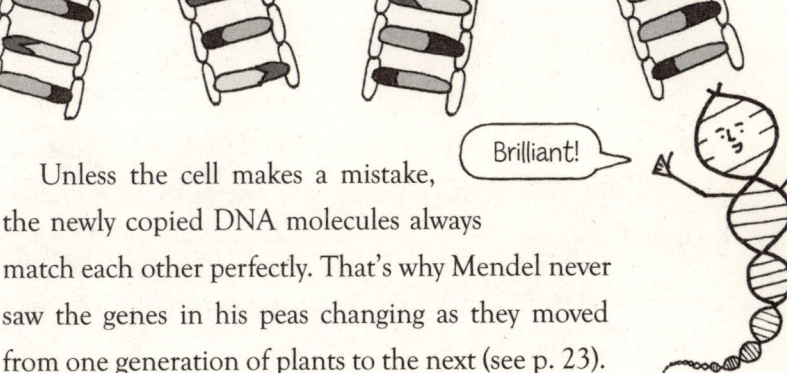

Unless the cell makes a mistake, the newly copied DNA molecules always match each other perfectly. That's why Mendel never saw the genes in his peas changing as they moved from one generation of plants to the next (see p. 23).

Brilliant!

Cells can go on churning out new copies of their genes and then dividing themselves as often as they like. Every newly made strand can act as a template for making yet more strands.

> And I thought I was a one-off.

Not so! There's a copy of you in nearly every cell in this reader's body. And in absolutely everyone else's bodies too – we all need haemoglobin in our blood. Between us all, humans carry **billions of trillions** of copies of Gene the gene.

If you tried to count up all the DNA molecules inside the cells of every other kind of creature, you'd end up with an even more bewilderingly, gobsmackingly, uncountably massive number. In short, DNA is a molecule that knows exactly how to spread itself, and the messages it contains, around the world. It does this because it wants – as much as a molecule can **want** anything – to make sure it will continue to exist far, far into the future.

But what do their nonsensical-looking messages actually say? And how do cells turn DNA instructions into the all-important proteins that spring into action inside our cells? That's what we'll find out next.

Hope you're ready, Gene, because you're the star of the next chapter.

> Whoop! Bring it on.

CHAPTER 3
DNA Takes Charge
WHY GENES ARE AT THE HEART OF EVERY LIVING CELL

Take a deep breath, because we're about to shrink ourselves down until we're much smaller than a cell. Then we're going to step into an actual human cell and see how it all works, from the inside*.

Prepare yourself to visit the busiest building site you could possibly imagine.

You'll see work going on absolutely everywhere. It's no exaggeration to say that the cell has its own versions of cement mixers, pneumatic drills, power saws, welders, electric cables, power generators, dumper trucks, diggers and much, much more.

Let's get TINY!

*For a more detailed experience of life inside a cell, see *Explodapedia: The Cell*.

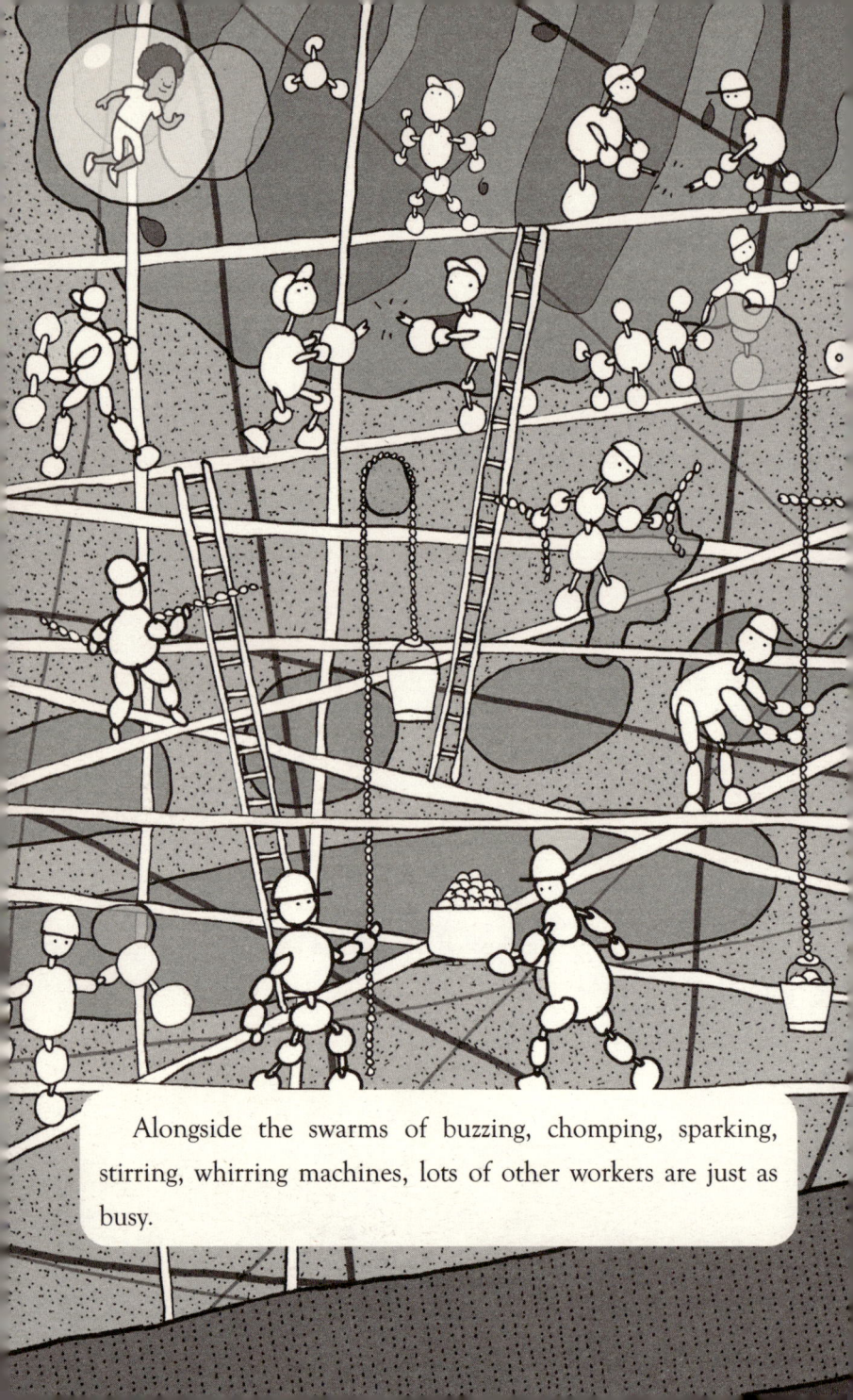

Alongside the swarms of buzzing, chomping, sparking, stirring, whirring machines, lots of other workers are just as busy.

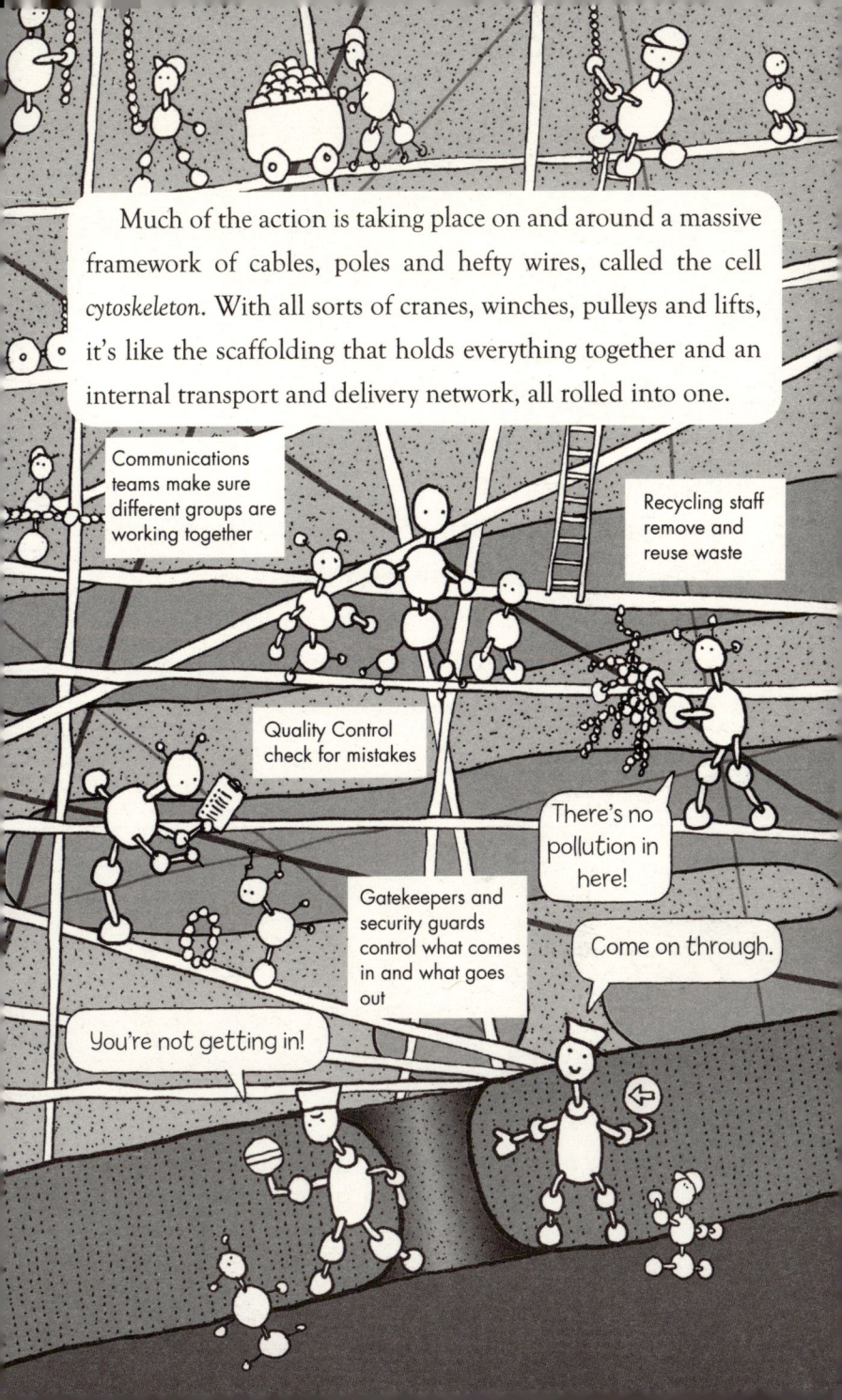

Much of the action is taking place on and around a massive framework of cables, poles and hefty wires, called the cell *cytoskeleton*. With all sorts of cranes, winches, pulleys and lifts, it's like the scaffolding that holds everything together and an internal transport and delivery network, all rolled into one.

Communications teams make sure different groups are working together

Recycling staff remove and reuse waste

Quality Control check for mistakes

There's no pollution in here!

Gatekeepers and security guards control what comes in and what goes out

Come on through.

You're not getting in!

Who's in Charge?

Don't mention tea breaks. This lot don't even stop for lunch, let alone to sleep. The cell is endlessly building, rebuilding and repairing itself. It's not that cells like this one need to grow any bigger, it's more that lots of jobs simply have to be done to keep a cell going. And as well as all that maintenance, a lot of cells can move themselves and change shape, sometimes quite dramatically, like when they reproduce by dividing in two.

The construction work inside a cell is incredibly well-run and efficient. There are millions of individual workers involved, and they all seem to know exactly what they have to do.

So, who, or what, is in charge of planning and running this insanely complex and never-ending building project?

At first sight, it might seem that the workers are in control. Most of them are made of protein, and many of the busiest among them are things called *enzymes*.

Cells usually contain hundreds of different kinds of enzyme and their job is to make, break or change all the thousands of different chemical substances cells need to stay alive. There'd be no life inside or outside the cell without them.

So are enzymes running the show?

> No way! **We're** in charge. Enzymes and all proteins are only here to serve DNA.

Gene might have a point there. The protein workers on the cell building project are good at what they do, but they aren't really making the decisions the way human workers would. They're more like pre-programmed robots, doing what they're told.

> And we're the ones that program them!

True, Gene. Those proteins are assembled and programmed according to the instructions spelled out in the genes' DNA. So, in some ways, genes really are in charge.

Don't let it go to your head, though, Gene. Because without all those proteins, you genes can't build anything, make energy, collect water or do any of the other things needed to keep cells going. To get **anything** done, your genes have to transform the information inside you into ACTION. And most of you do that by making the proteins that do all this work.

Turning Information into Action

There's no escaping the fact that making pre-programmed proteins to do the genes' work is quite a complicated process. It involves DNA and a similar substance called *ribonucleic acid (RNA)*. Like DNA, RNA is made up of four nucleotide letters that spell out a chemical code.

We know that DNA code is: **ATGC**
RNA code is only one letter different: **AUGC**[*]

There are two types of RNA at the centre of the action:
- *Messenger RNA*, mRNA for short, is basically a **messenger** for the genes.
- *Transfer RNA*, tRNA for short, **transfers** the gene's information into a new protein molecule.

We can break the whole process down into three main stages. Let's take Gene with us as we find out more.

I'm up for that!

[*] RNA uses a nucleotide called U (which stands for uracil) in place of DNA's T (thymine).

STAGE 1. TRANSCRIPTION: TURNING DNA INTO RNA

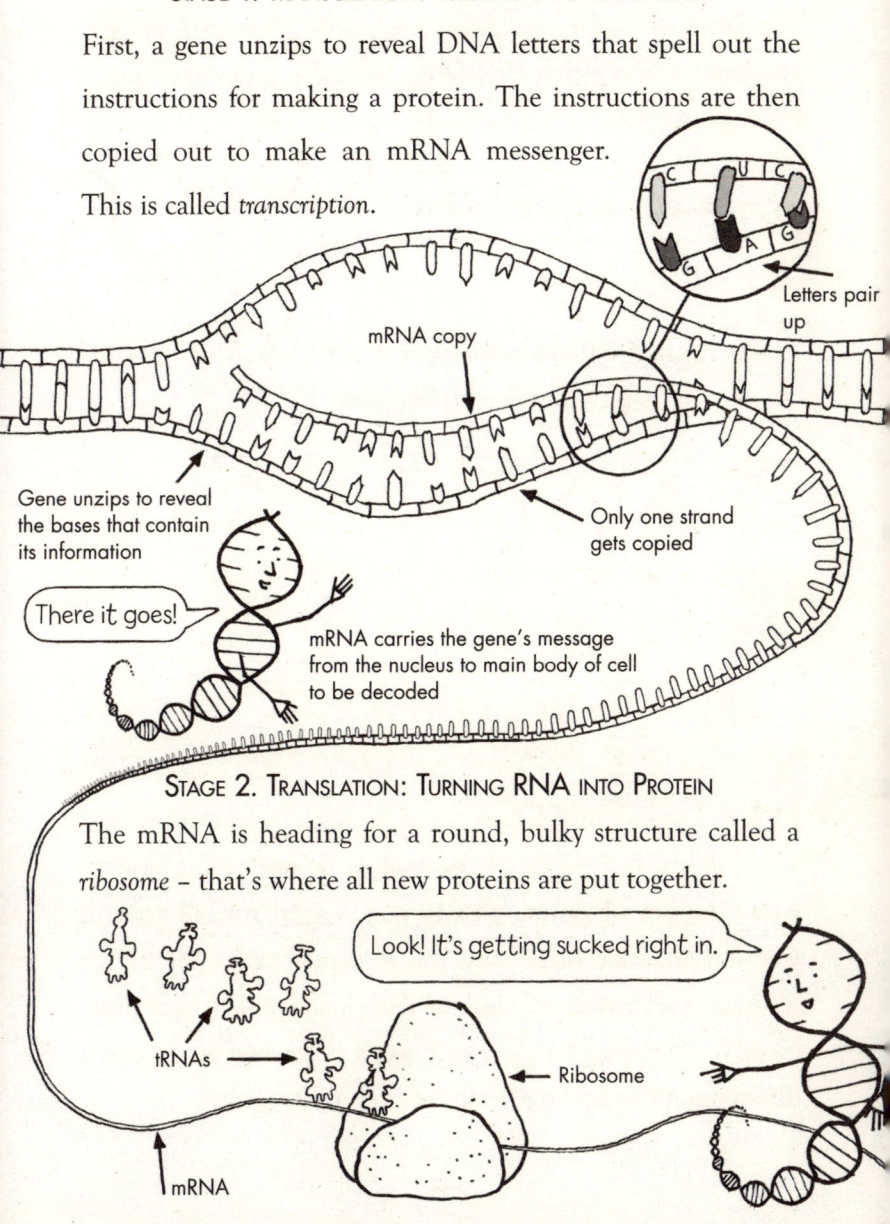

First, a gene unzips to reveal DNA letters that spell out the instructions for making a protein. The instructions are then copied out to make an mRNA messenger. This is called *transcription*.

Letters pair up

mRNA copy

Gene unzips to reveal the bases that contain its information

Only one strand gets copied

There it goes!

mRNA carries the gene's message from the nucleus to main body of cell to be decoded

STAGE 2. TRANSLATION: TURNING RNA INTO PROTEIN

The mRNA is heading for a round, bulky structure called a *ribosome* – that's where all new proteins are put together.

Look! It's getting sucked right in.

tRNAs

Ribosome

mRNA

So, what does the ribosome actually do? Well, while RNA and DNA speak the same language – gene language – protein language is completely different. To make a protein, gene's instructions have to be *translated*.

> I can't understand a thing proteins say.

There are **twenty** letters in the protein code. They're called *amino acids*, and they look a bit like this:

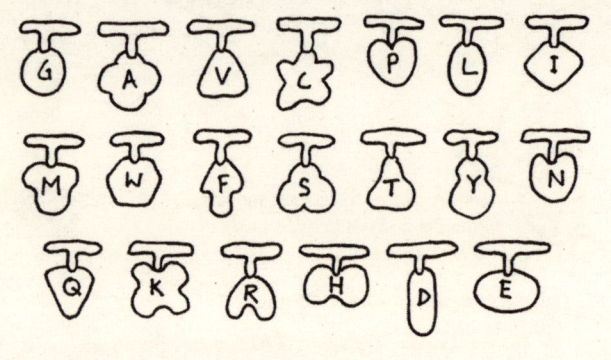

These amino acid letters are each carried around by their own kind of transfer RNA. As well as delivering the protein letters to the ribosome, tRNAs play a vital role in protein translation. They make sure the ribosome reads the gene's message three letters at a time, as if it's made up of lots of short 'words'. Then they translate each word of gene language into a different amino acid (or 'letter' of protein language).

Let's take a closer look at one of them to see how they do it:

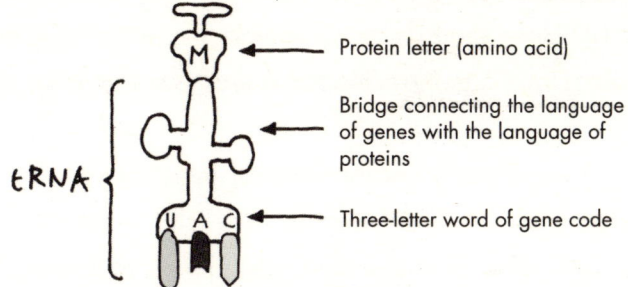

- Protein letter (amino acid)
- Bridge connecting the language of genes with the language of proteins
- Three-letter word of gene code

tRNA

This all comes together inside the ribosome:

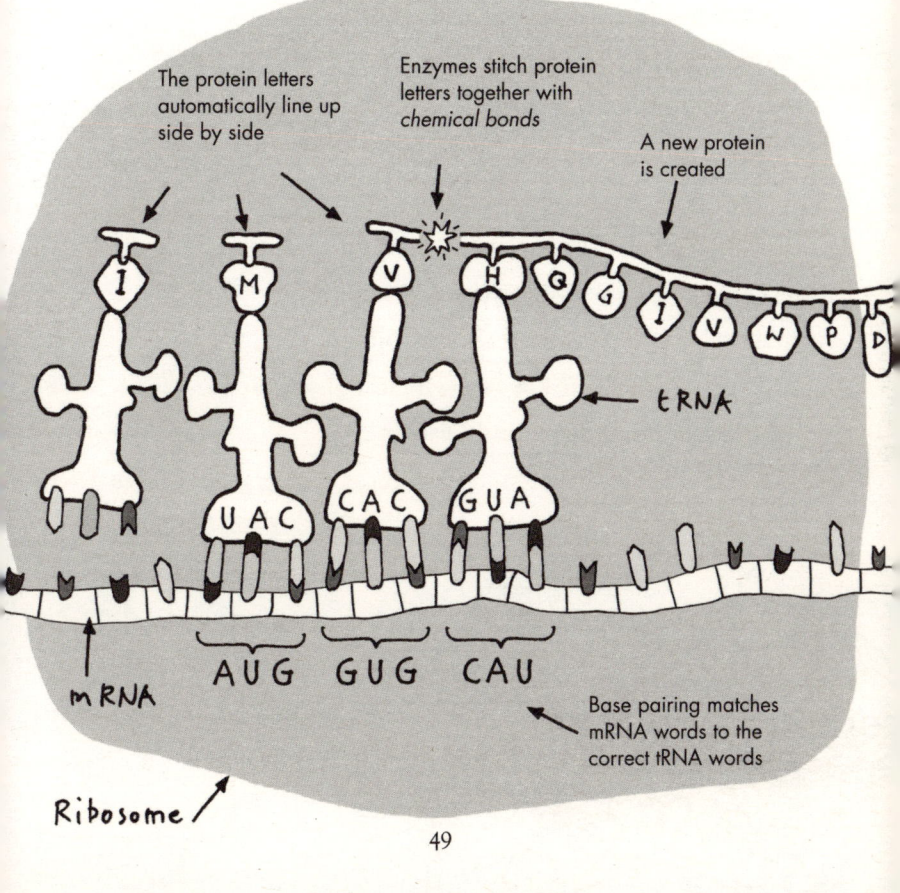

- The protein letters automatically line up side by side
- Enzymes stitch protein letters together with *chemical bonds*
- A new protein is created
- tRNA
- mRNA
- Base pairing matches mRNA words to the correct tRNA words
- Ribosome

49

The shiny new protein that comes out of the other side of the ribosome can't do much at first. It's just a long, wriggly chain of linked amino acids. But it won't stay that way for long.

Stage 3. Protein Folding: Taking Shape

Protein molecules look amazing. After they emerge from the ribosome, they twist and turn into all sorts of shapes. To do their jobs, proteins must be able to bind to other molecules in very specific ways. They have to form precise shapes, a bit like tiny 'keys' that slip in and out of tiny 'locks'.

How do proteins get into these shapes? Well, the gene tells the amino acids the order they should take in the protein chain. Then the amino acids in the chain tell a protein how it should fold up.

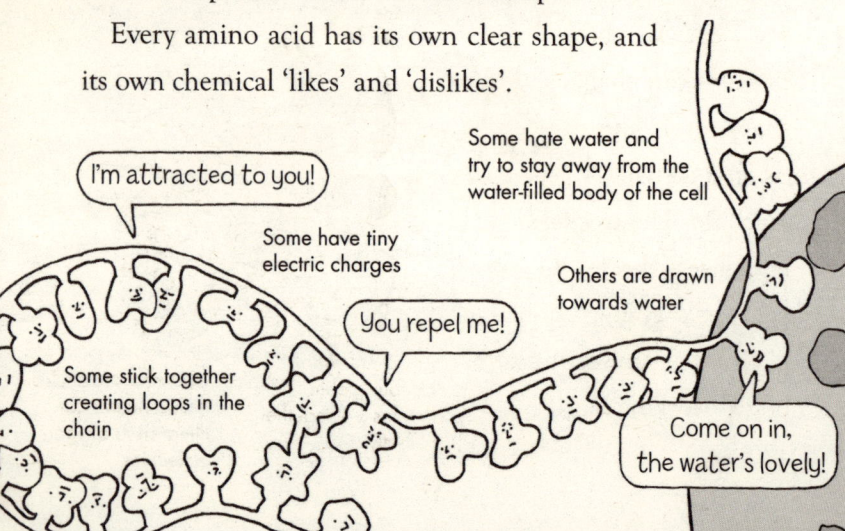

Every amino acid has its own clear shape, and its own chemical 'likes' and 'dislikes'.

I'm attracted to you!

Some have tiny electric charges

Some hate water and try to stay away from the water-filled body of the cell

Others are drawn towards water

You repel me!

Some stick together creating loops in the chain

Come on in, the water's lovely!

It's the combination of amino acids in newly made protein chains that cause different parts of it to coil, scrunch, bend, pleat, turn or twist, eventually making finished proteins with all sorts of weird and wonderful shapes.

Lots of proteins can hinge, bend and flex to do their work. Actually, that's an important feature of the protein that Gene makes.

Gene's been working on an invention for millions of years. Want to share it with us, Gene?

Hell, yes!

Gene's Masterpiece

Your red blood cells are jam-packed with Gene's haemoglobin, which carries oxygen around your body. And because of the way haemoglobin's proteins can change shape, it is the perfect oxygen-transporting machine. The oxygen it delivers keeps all of your cells going, but it's particularly useful if your body's working hard.

Haemoglobin is made from four different proteins called *globins*. Gene makes half of them

The four globin proteins slot together perfectly

Chemical molecules called *haems* can cling on to oxygen molecules

Here's what happens when you're running for a bus:

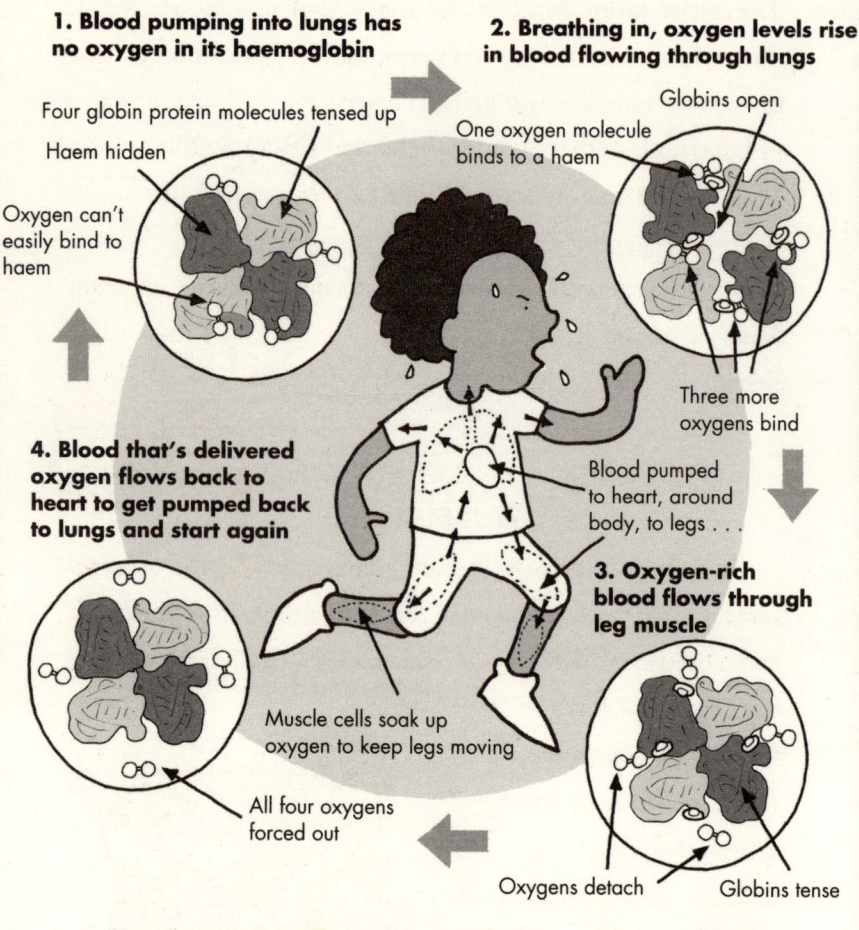

1. Blood pumping into lungs has no oxygen in its haemoglobin

Four globin protein molecules tensed up
Haem hidden
Oxygen can't easily bind to haem

2. Breathing in, oxygen levels rise in blood flowing through lungs

Globins open
One oxygen molecule binds to a haem
Three more oxygens bind

Blood pumped to heart, around body, to legs . . .

3. Oxygen-rich blood flows through leg muscle

Muscle cells soak up oxygen to keep legs moving

Oxygens detach
Globins tense

4. Blood that's delivered oxygen flows back to heart to get pumped back to lungs and start again

All four oxygens forced out

Gene's ingenious design means that the cells in our bodies never have to ask for more oxygen. Haemoglobin makes sure it just arrives automatically, when and where it's needed.

> It is quite clever, even if I say so myself.

Your Cells Are Crammed with Mini Masterpieces

The cell building site we saw on pages 42–43 contained 20,000 different protein-making genes. So, like every other cell in our bodies, it can get jobs done by choosing from a huge variety of protein workers that each have their own unique skills and are all just as carefully crafted as Gene's haemoglobin protein.

A single gene can also make the same protein over and over again, to construct a whole army of identical workers and really make sure a job gets done. For example, a single red blood cell contains a whopping **270 million** haemoglobins[*].

On the other hand, the workers made by some genes aren't proteins at all. For example, certain enzymes that work in the ribosomes are made from RNA.

Together, these busy hordes of genes, RNAs and proteins keep the inner workings of a cell better organized and more complex than anything a human inventor could even dream of. So perhaps the most amazing thing about it is that nothing that's even vaguely intelligent . . .

Hey, don't be rude!

. . . is involved in designing or running the cell. Working together with its genes, a cell does everything for itself.

[*] That's almost as many protein machines as there are people in the USA!

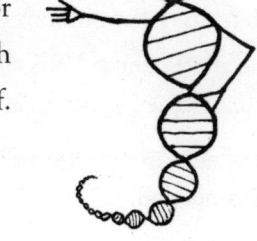

CHAPTER 4
Cooking Up a Human
Why Genes Mean We're all Basically the Same

Before a house can be built, an architect has to draw up a set of plans. When the construction workers come to build the house, those plans tell them exactly how to do it. The walls must be built with bricks; it must be two storeys tall; have three bedrooms, twelve windows, eight doors, and so on. Usually, everything is spelled out in great detail, including where the electric sockets go and what kind of handle should go on the bathroom door.

There's no master plan for building a human. Your DNA definitely contains the instructions needed to make you, but no matter how hard scientists scrutinize DNA code, they will never find a gene that's in charge of making your left ear or an instruction for how many eyelashes you should have.

There are no builders involved either. Your body built **itself**. Gradually, painstakingly - almost unbelievably - the little fertilized egg cell that started you off grew into the fully formed baby that came squirming and shrieking into the world about nine months later. Your mother's body helped you through this process - it protected you, kept you stocked with nutrients, oxygen and water, and even took away your waste - but it was always supporting you, never in charge. It was **your** body, made from **your** cells, containing **your** genes, that did all the construction work needed to put **you** together.

GENES ARE INGREDIENTS FOR BAKING CELLS

So if genes don't work like an architect's blueprints, are they following a recipe instead?

Not quite. But the complete set of genes in every one of your cells is a bit like a gigantic list of possible cooking ingredients. Those genes make protein and RNA molecules that can be used to cook up a massive range of tasty dishes. The dishes are your cells, and your body contains hundreds of different kinds, each with their own shape, size and way of working.

The cells in your body are born with the same list of possible gene 'ingredients', but they each have their own special recipe. Just as pizza and cake have different ingredients, the cells in your blood, muscles and brain each use **some** gene ingredients and ignore the rest. Hence they all work differently.

In a process called *differentiation*, cells are changed, by using some genes and ignoring all others. By switching the right genes 'on' at the right moment:

• Red blood cells fill themselves up with lots of oxygen-carrying haemoglobin.

- Muscle cells grow fibres that contract and relax.
- Brain cells make incredibly long, thin connections that wire up your brain and body.

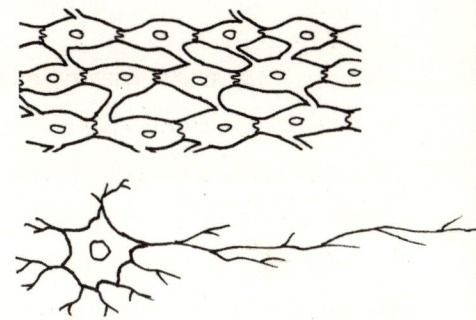

Let's think about chocolate cake. Mmm... When you bake it, all the different ingredients blend together. It's not as if the eggs control how fluffy the crumbs are, the flour's in charge of making the cake moist and the sugar takes control of the flavour. You only get a tasty cake if you mix the ingredients in just the right way and cook them for the right amount of time. It's the same with genes: picking the right combination of genes, and mixing them just right, is absolutely essential.

There's no head chef in the cell kitchen, though. And recipes for cells are far, far more complicated than any you'll find in a cookbook.

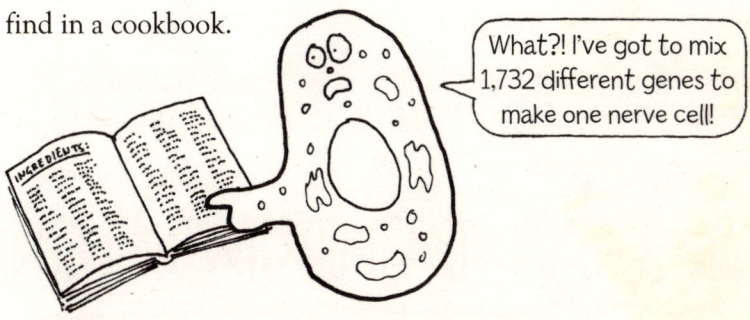

What?! I've got to mix 1,732 different genes to make one nerve cell!

What's more, cells are never really fully 'cooked'. From the moment they're created to the moment they die, they're repairing themselves, changing shape and responding as the world changes around them. That means they're always adding and removing gene ingredients, and changing their inner workings.

So if there's no cook in the cell kitchen, what's choosing the genes that a cell must use? It's time to get to know some *transcription factors*.

Turning the Right Genes On and the Wrong Genes Off

Transcription factors are special proteins that can turn genes 'on' and 'off'. They work by binding to pieces of DNA called *regulatory sequences*. These pieces of DNA don't hold the information for making protein or RNA; instead, they control when the gene is used. When a transcription factor latches onto a regulatory sequence, the two act together as a switch. They can turn nearby genes 'on', like this:

Transcription factor switches gene 'on'

RNA starts making protein

Gene starts making mRNA

Regulatory sequences

Gene

Or they can turn genes 'off', like this:

Transcription factor switches gene 'off'

Gene stops making mRNA

Regulatory sequences

Gene

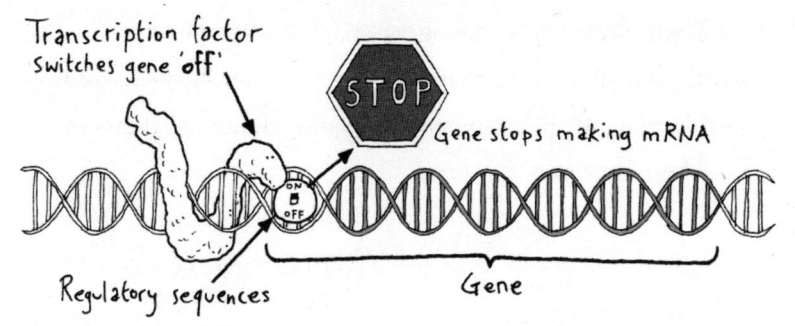

Things would go badly wrong if blood cells started flipping on the wrong genes.

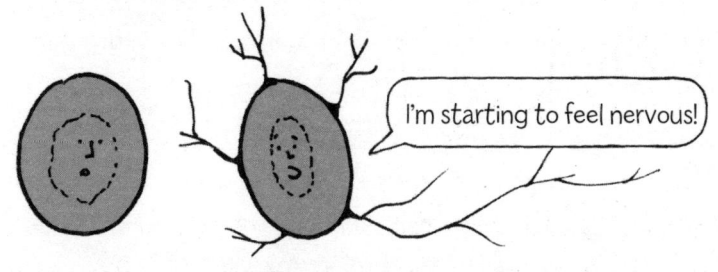

I'm starting to feel nervous!

So cell differentiation is all about having the right transcription factors in the right place at the right time.

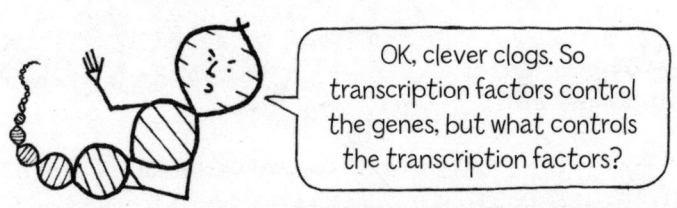

OK, clever clogs. So transcription factors control the genes, but what controls the transcription factors?

Now you're asking. Partly it's other transcription factors. Your cells contain genes for making hundreds of different transcription factors, and they can flip each other's genes 'on' and 'off'.

Then there are signals coming from **outside** the cell. The different cells in your body are constantly communicating with each other, using things called *signalling molecules*.

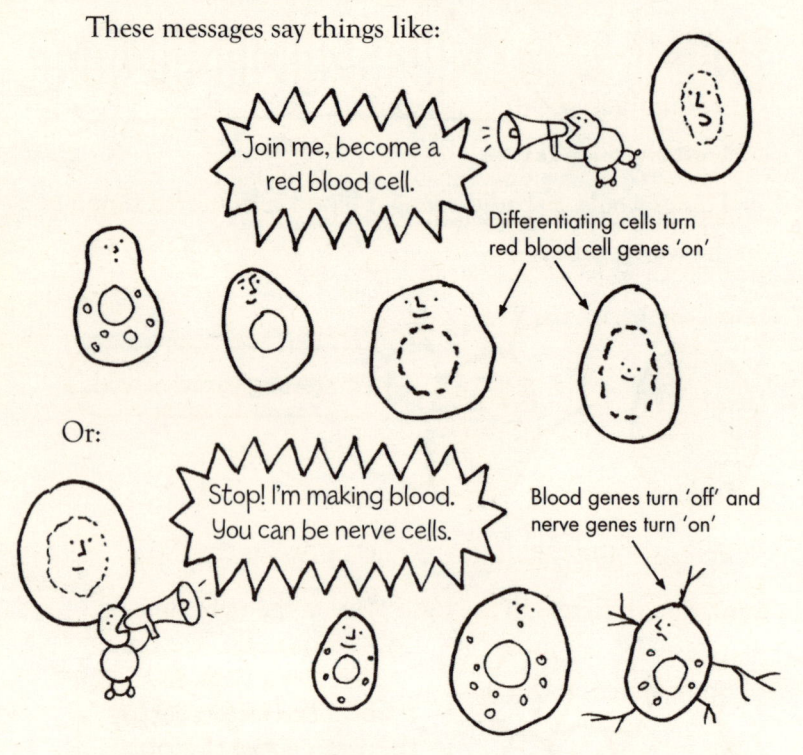

These messages say things like:

Join me, become a red blood cell.

Differentiating cells turn red blood cell genes 'on'

Or:

Stop! I'm making blood. You can be nerve cells.

Blood genes turn 'off' and nerve genes turn 'on'

There's no perfect way of describing how cells use their DNA code to build a fully formed baby. It's a **bit** like a building project; it's a **bit** like cooking; you could even say it's a **bit** like computer programming. But it's not completely like any of them. It's unique and it's extraordinary, but at the same time it's kind of ordinary – after all, it's a process we've all been through, and the reason you're here today, reading these words.

Biologists still have a lot to learn about how it all happens. They have at least worked out that the DNA inside every new cell contains instructions for making:

• **Hundreds** of transcription factors that switch genes 'on' or 'off'.

• **Hundreds of thousands** of regulatory sequences that link the right transcription factors to the right genes.

• **Dozens** of different signalling molecules that allow them to instruct each other to differentiate.

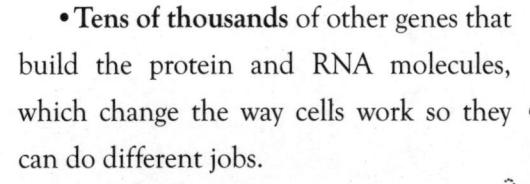

• **Tens of thousands** of other genes that build the protein and RNA molecules, which change the way cells work so they can do different jobs.

Like me and my haemoglobin!

So, those are the basic facts you need to know. Now let's see how they work during some of the most important stages in the long journey a zygote takes to become a baby.

266 Days to Make a Human: The Highlights

Day 1. The Zygote It's just a single, lonely cell, but a baby is made from umpteen million cells, so it has to get dividing, fast.

Transcription factors trigger genes that make this cell reproduce itself

Day 3. The Morula It's a blob of 16 cells that look pretty much identical. To make a baby, some of them are going to have to start differentiating. These first changes are vital – like the first domino falling in a domino rally, they trigger all the other stages of cell differentiation.

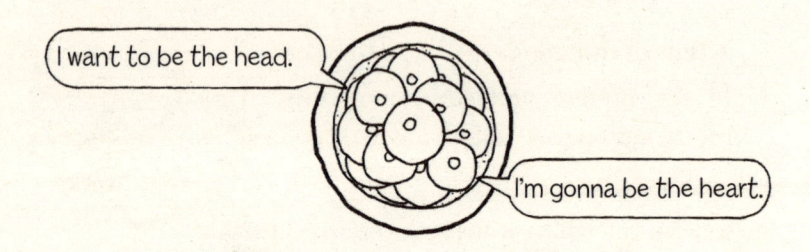

I want to be the head.

I'm gonna be the heart.

Day 6. The Blastocyst Finally, there's some clear pattern emerging! The cells on the outside are going to build the placenta, which will connect the growing baby to its mother's womb. The baby's entire body will develop from the cluster of cells on the inside, called the inner cell mass.

Outside – cells make placenta

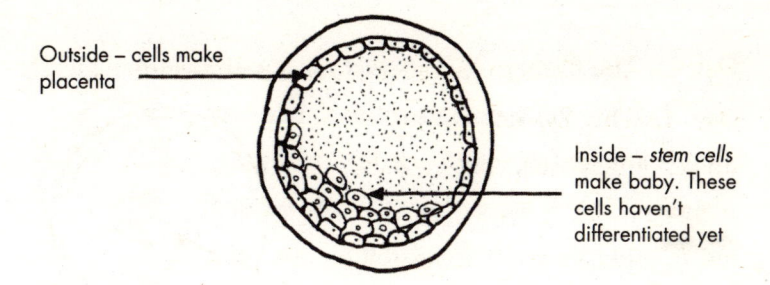

Inside – *stem cells* make baby. These cells haven't differentiated yet

Day 12. The Embryonic Disc The fast-growing ball of cells has embedded itself in the mother's womb. The inner cell mass has changed through differentiation and is now made up of three different kinds of cell:

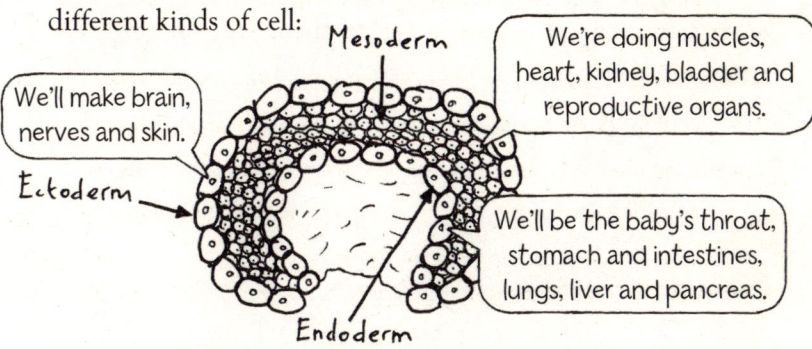

Mesoderm

We're doing muscles, heart, kidney, bladder and reproductive organs.

We'll make brain, nerves and skin.

Ectoderm

We'll be the baby's throat, stomach and intestines, lungs, liver and pancreas.

Endoderm

From now on their paths are set, so no *endoderm* or *mesoderm* cell will ever turn itself into a brain cell, and no *ectoderm* or mesoderm cell will ever make part of the liver, etc.

Actually, that's not quite true!

In 2007, stem cell expert, Shinya Yamanaka, proved that switching 'on' just four transcription factors in almost any adult cell is enough to turn it back into a stem cell.

Day 42. The *Embryo* Is it an alien? Is it a weird-looking teddy bear? No, it's still a human embryo, but now things are getting even more interesting. There's clearly a head, there's a tiny beating heart and those little nubbins are the beginnings of arms and legs.

It's a Boy!

Around this time, something very important happens, but only in boys. Sons inherit a single transcription factor, called SRY, from their fathers that gets switched 'on' now. And that's all it takes to trigger the growth of testicles and all the other features that will eventually make a male baby. If it wasn't for this transcription factor, all babies would be female.*

Day 70. The *Foetus* It looks much more recognizably human. That's definitely a face, and all the body's main organs have taken shape. Now it's time to work on the finer details, like eyelids and earlobes.

---

*Biological sex, i.e. whether someone is born with a male or female body, is not always the same as gender identity.

Day 168. The Baby Most babies keep growing in the womb for another three months, but by this point nearly all of the main cell types have already differentiated. If the baby was born now, with the right medical care, it would have a great chance of surviving and living a healthy life. It can suck its thumb and its sense organs are well developed – it can even hear music playing in the world outside.

Around Day 266. The Newborn Woohoo! It's time to say 'Hello World!' One lonely little zygote cell has used its own DNA code to divide and differentiate itself to make around **two trillion cells** (that's about six times more cells than there are stars in our entire galaxy). And, together, those cells can shout, wriggle, suckle and learn.

Whatever colour this baby's eyes are, whatever shade its skin and hair, whether it's male or female, big or small, it is most definitely a human being. Putting it all together is the most important thing its genes will ever do.

While the parents will be convinced their cherub is special, probably the most amazing thing about babies is that they are all basically the same. And there's a very good reason for that: all human beings contain an **almost** identical set of genes – they're the genes that make us humans (instead of chimpanzees, chickens or cherry trees).

But that word 'almost' is important. Your genes aren't quite identical to anyone else's. Over the next couple of chapters we're going to find out how that came to be and why it matters.

CHAPTER 5
Meet Your Genome
THE GENES, THE JUNK AND THE GIGANTIC CHROMOSOMES

You inherited all of your genes at the very start of your life. One complete set came from your mother's egg cell. They were spread out along 23 separate pieces of DNA called *chromosomes*. Then, when your father's sperm cell fertilized that egg, it delivered a matching set of genes, inside a matching set of 23 chromosomes. In total, your parents gave you a full set of 46 chromosomes. All your genes came in pairs – just as Mendel said they would (see p. 22). The 23rd pair are the sex chromosomes (see p. 84). Together, all your chromosomes, containing all your genes, is called your *genome**.

---

*As well as the main set of 46 chromosomes, everyone inherits a small number of extra genes from their mum's egg cell. They're found inside structures called *mitochondria*, which make energy for your cells.

Chromosomes are often drawn as neat little X shapes, like this:

XX XX XX XX XX
XX XX XX XX XX XX XX
XX XX XX XX XX XX
XX XX XX XX X Y

Each chromosome is a long piece of DNA wrapped round thousands of tiny protein 'spools'

Pair 23 consists of an X and a Y chromosome in males and two X chromosomes in females (more on this in Chapter 6)

That's how chromosomes look while cells are in the process of dividing themselves. The rest of the time, they're more like this:

Actually, the DNA pieces that make up your chromosomes are some of the longest molecules in the known universe. If we stretched out all the DNA molecules that are packed up inside each minuscule cell in a boy's body here's how long they'd be:

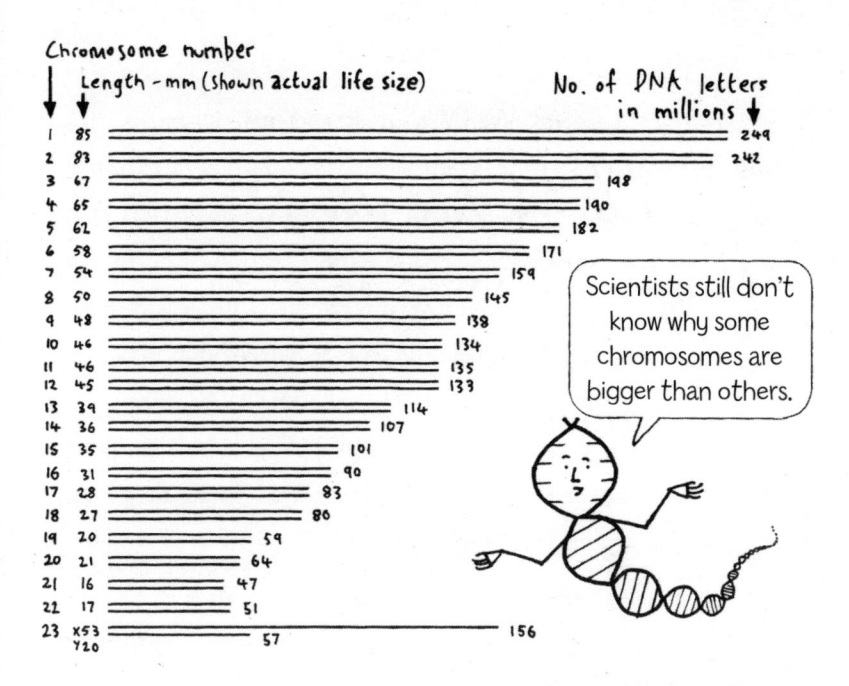

Chromosome number
↓ Length - mm (shown actual life size)   No. of DNA letters in millions ↓

#	Length (mm)	DNA letters (millions)
1	85	249
2	83	242
3	67	198
4	65	190
5	62	182
6	58	171
7	54	159
8	50	145
9	48	138
10	46	134
11	46	135
12	45	133
13	39	114
14	36	107
15	35	101
16	31	90
17	28	83
18	27	86
19	20	59
20	21	64
21	16	47
22	17	51
23	X 53 / Y 20	156 / 57

Scientists still don't know why some chromosomes are bigger than others.

If you joined all those chromosome lines together end to end, you'd see that your complete genome is an amazing **two metres long**. That's because the chromosomes are jam-packed with a stupendous amount of code - 6.2 billion DNA letters of it, in fact.

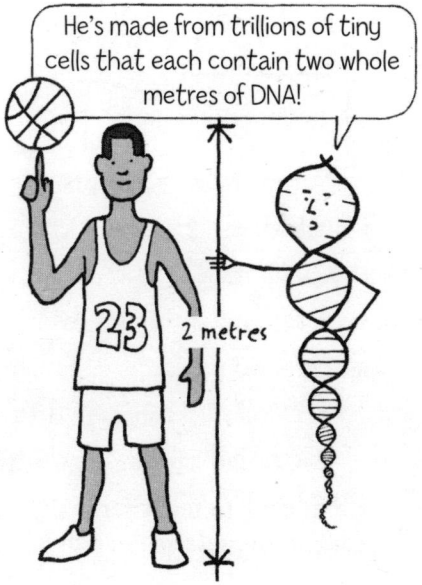

He's made from trillions of tiny cells that each contain two whole metres of DNA!

2 metres

69

GENES: WE WANT TO READ YOU!

Ever since Mendel's time, scientists had been desperate to find out what messages genes contain. But it wasn't until 1977 that a British scientist called Fred Sanger finally managed to invent a chemical process that let him 'read' the nucleotide 'letters' that make up a piece of DNA. He called it *DNA sequencing*.

This was a pretty amazing breakthrough, but using it to sequence an **entire** human genome was going to be an extremely slow and very boring task.

> I sequenced 500 letters of DNA today, boss.

> Excellent. At that rate you'll complete the patient's genome in... **17,000 years**.

Surprisingly, scientists weren't put off. Instead, they launched the Human Genome Project in 1990. To speed things up they:

• Recruited thousands of scientists, working in dozens of labs around world.

• Developed robots to do a lot of the really boring tasks.

• Created cutting-edge software, which ran on massive computers, to make sense of the results.

And it worked.

But it still took until 2003 to churn through that first human genome. Nowadays, Sanger's original process has been replaced by much faster methods and the computers that crunch that data are far more powerful – one scientist, working alone, can do someone's entire genome in just one day.

Even so, sequencing that first genome was a massive achievement. Biologists could finally see what our DNA code actually said. But they were in for a shock.

Where Are All the Genes?

Ever seen a walrus writing poetry, a baboon building a rocket, or a banana tree giving a lecture? Thought not. Humans are exceptionally imaginative and intelligent animals, so you'd think (and so would a lot of scientists) we must be the most sophisticated animals of all. It came as a huge surprise when the project showed that the human **genome** doesn't contain all that many **genes**.

> Tiny see-through water fleas have 31,000 genes that make proteins. And this grain of wheat has 95,000 of them.

> We humans have only got 20,000 protein-making genes.

> So, clearly, it's not the total number of genes that counts; it's how you use them.

AND WHAT'S ALL THIS JUNK?

The second revelation was even more disturbing: most of the human genome wasn't made up of genes at all. Some biologists already expected that would be true, but none of them predicted that quite so much of our precious DNA would appear to contain NO USEFUL INFORMATION WHATSOEVER!

If all the DNA letters in your genome were grouped together on the basis of what they do inside your cells, and then printed in separate books, here's what those books would look like:

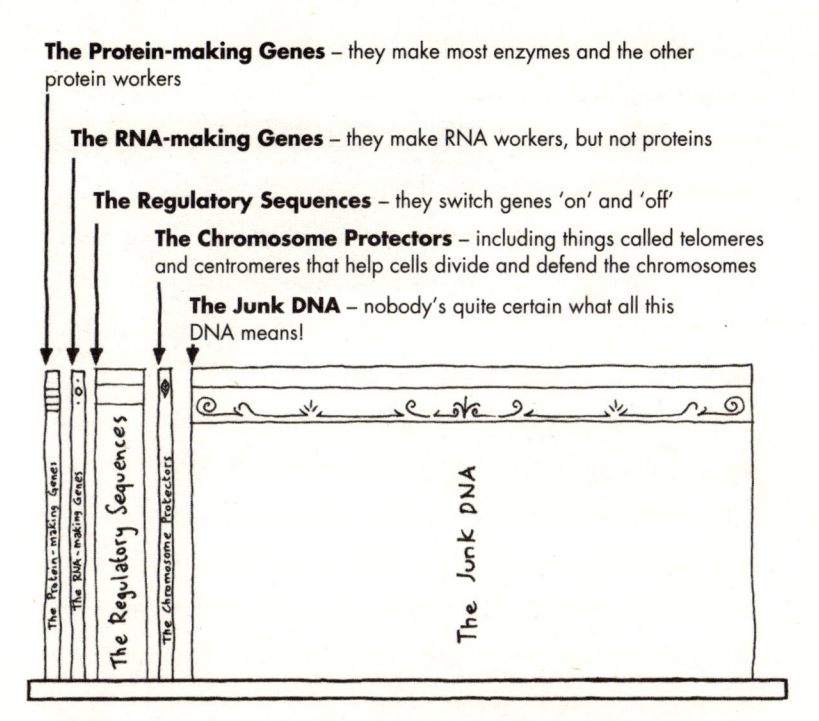

The Protein-making Genes – they make most enzymes and the other protein workers

The RNA-making Genes – they make RNA workers, but not proteins

The Regulatory Sequences – they switch genes 'on' and 'off'

The Chromosome Protectors – including things called telomeres and centromeres that help cells divide and defend the chromosomes

The Junk DNA – nobody's quite certain what all this DNA means!

The first thing you'll notice is that *The Junk DNA* is ridiculously massive! And, alarmingly, if you looked inside, you'd see that most of it reads as gibberish.

For example:

A lot of it is made up of the same meaningless sentences, printed again and again. A lot of it is made up of the same meaningless sentences, printed again and again. A lot of it is made up of the same meaningless sentences, printed again and again. A lot of it is made up of the same meaningless sentences, printed again and again. A lot of it is made up of the same meaningless sentences, printed again and again. A lot of it is made up of the same meaningless sentences, printed again and again.

Chunks of nonsense DNA a bit like this are sometimes repeated **millions** of times.

Some of this junk DNA is almost certainly there for a reason; scientists just haven't worked out what that reason is yet.

What we do know is that quite a lot of junk DNA sequences were put there by viruses that infected your pre-human *ancestors* millions of years ago! Those viruses were parasites – all they wanted to do was get themselves replicated.

The same is true for things called *transposable elements*, which make up an even bigger share of junk DNA. They've got no interest in helping us; they just want to make sure our cells copy them, which is why they're sometimes called *selfish DNA*. Some transposable elements behave as if they have a will of their own; they can actually jump from one chromosome to another, multiplying as they go.

They've done that a lot in the past: so often, in fact, that nearly **half** of the total amount of DNA in your chromosomes consists of transposable elements.

> Count yourself lucky. My genome's 14 times bigger than a human's, and it's mostly junk DNA.

Australian lungfish

Somehow It All Still Works!

If your genome really was printed in a set of books, it wouldn't actually be organized into neat volumes, like the example on page 73. In reality, it's all completely mixed up. And if the genes and their regulatory sequences contain the main plot of the human story, they've been separated from each other and scattered around, willy-nilly, among page after page of incomprehensible codswallop.

Even the genes themselves get interrupted by random strings of DNA letters called *introns*. So if this sentence was a gene:

I MAKE A SHINY NEW PROTEIN.

Its introns would make it much harder to read, like this:

I MAKE A WVMIRSNFGY SHINY DZVHLGMXBZ NEW PROWJAYTENIFPTEIN.

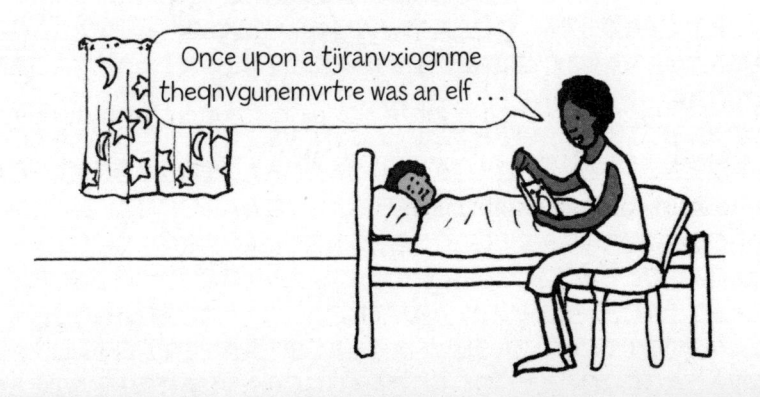

> Once upon a tijranvxiognme theqnvgunemvrtre was an elf...

Except, if it was a real gene, spotting the useful bits would be even trickier, since both the gene and the introns consist of nothing but As, Ts, Cs and Gs!

In fact, it's amazing biologists have been able to make sense of any of this DNA code. And even more amazing that our precious genes still work, despite being completely surrounded, and interrupted, by so much apparently meaningless DNA drivel, which was mostly put there by selfish parasites!

Those genes definitely do still work though. Between them all, they contain the information for building both an average human – the kind with four limbs, two ears, one nose and a heart that beats – **and** the extraordinary human, otherwise known as you.

Next, we'll find out how; by seeing how genes can change and why that means your genome isn't quite like anyone else's.

CHAPTER 6
Mutant Invasion!
How Your Genes Make You Truly Unique

When it comes to genes, Mendel got a lot of things right. But he was wrong when he said genes **never** change (see p. 23).

Oh really? Tell me more?

For three main reasons, actually:

1. **Mistakes** Every now and then cells mis-copy individual letters, add extra ones in, or miss them out completely. Occasionally, whole chunks of DNA get accidentally skipped over, copied twice or moved from one chromosome to another.

2. **Damage** Certain poisonous chemicals and some kinds of radiation – including getting too much sunlight – can get into cells and damage their genes.

3. **Virus genes and transposable elements** These junk DNA sequences (see p. 74) can 'hop' from one part of the genome to another, changing gene codes as they do so.

> Amazing. Scientists **have** been busy since my day.

Overall, mistakes and mishaps are rare, and cells work hard to put them right. But when changes to DNA become permanent, biologists call them *mutations*. Every cell that contains a new mutation will pass it on every time it divides. And, as we'll see, the effects those changes have on egg and sperm cells that become the next generation can range from very useful, to catastrophically awful, to nothing at all.

We're All Mutants

Small mutations that only change one letter of DNA are the most common sort. They're kind of like typos in a text message, except, on average, there's just **one** 'typo' for every **10 billion** new DNA letters your cells 'write'. Imagine tapping out 100,000 copies of this entire book and only hitting **one** wrong key.

There are bigger mutations that affect more DNA letters, but they happen even less often.

Individual mutations are rare, but they add up over the generations. Mutations that altered your ancestor's genomes got passed down to more recent relatives and eventually to you. With every generation a few dozen new mutations are added to the mix.

> Hang on. If we all inherit loads of mutations... are we all mutants?

Well, yes we are, but that doesn't mean we've all got amazing powers, like the X-Men. A gene mutation is just a change in the sequence of a piece of DNA. Which is why most biologists prefer to call them *genetic variants*, or just *variants*. Everyone's genome contains a totally unique set of variants.

These days scientists can scan anyone's genome and spot all the different variants. If you lined up your DNA side by side with a random, unrelated stranger's and looked across all the chromosomes, there'd be an average of:

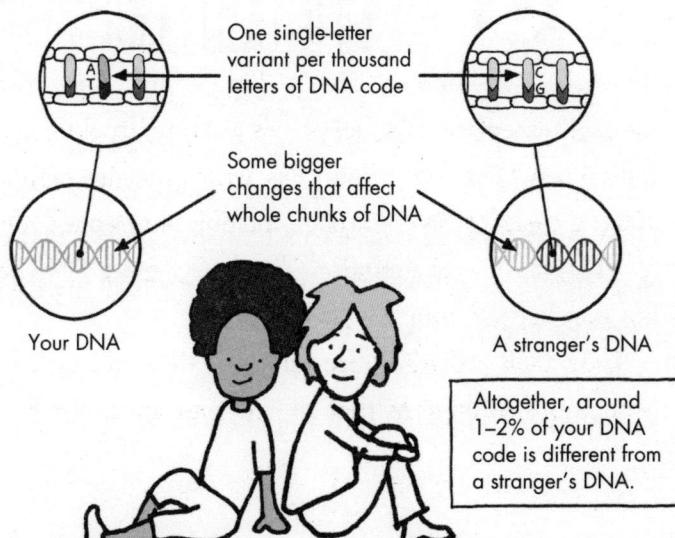

One single-letter variant per thousand letters of DNA code

Some bigger changes that affect whole chunks of DNA

Your DNA

A stranger's DNA

Altogether, around 1–2% of your DNA code is different from a stranger's DNA.

If you then compared your DNA with a **different** stranger's DNA, you'd see a similar thing: 1–2% of the code would not match. But most of those variants would show up in different parts of your chromosomes. We've all got our own distinctive pattern, like a kind of DNA-based barcode.

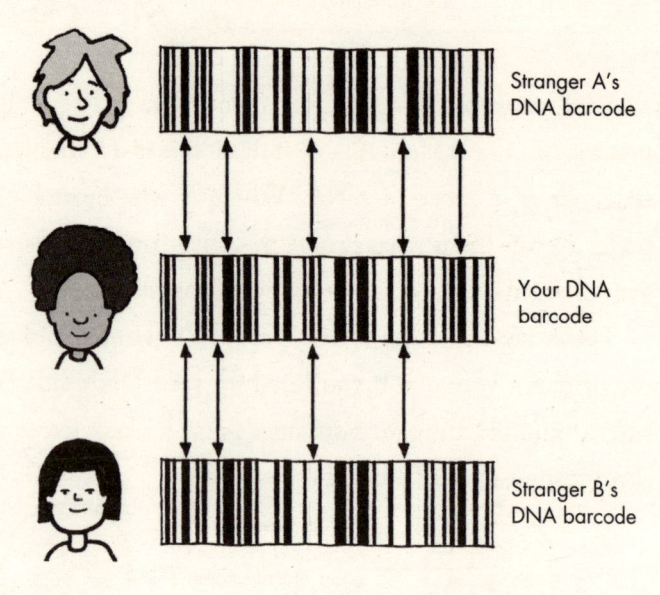

Stranger A's DNA barcode

Your DNA barcode

Stranger B's DNA barcode

In fact, if any two people on the whole planet compared their genomes, they'd be at least 98% identical. That matching DNA is the code that makes us human. The fact that we all share so much is proof that we're far more similar to each other than we sometimes like to think.

It also means that only 2%, at most, of your genome is genuinely unique to **you**. But then, your genome is truly massive, so that tiny percentage adds up to a whopping **60–100 million** letters-worth of DNA difference – 600 times the total number of letters in this whole book! And that's enough variants to affect the way your genes work and have a huge impact on your life.

Why Your Brother Is Like No Other

Of course, your immediate family have a DNA code that's usually much more similar to yours than yours is to any random stranger's.

But if you have brothers or sisters, you'll already know that you're different from your siblings and have been since the moment you were born – even though you inherited your genes from the same two parents:

Mum's fast legs, Dad's curly hair and love of dogs

Dad's curly hair, green eyes and Mum's quick wit

Mum's straight hair and Dad's cheeky sense of humour

Imagine that the complete set of variants in each parent's genome is a pack of playing cards. It's as if each parent 'shuffled' them up and 'dealt' each child a different 'hand' of gene variants. All living things that reproduce sexually (see p. 16) do this. It's a way of making sure that all the offspring two parents have (apart from identical twins, triplets etc.) are slightly different. So some of those children stand a better chance of surviving and thriving if the world suddenly makes life tougher.

That shuffling and dealing of genes happens during a special kind of cell division, called *meiosis*, which makes *sex cells* (sperm cells in males and egg cells in females).

Each sex cell contains one set of 23 chromosomes, rather than the usual two sets. That way, when sperm and egg fuse to kickstart a new life, the fertilized egg cell has the 46 chromosomes it needs.

Meiosis also jumbles the chromosomes up. It's an insanely complicated process, but here's roughly how it happened when a cell in your mum's ovaries made the egg cell that eventually became you. To keep it simple, we'll focus on **just one pair of chromosomes**, rather than the full 23:

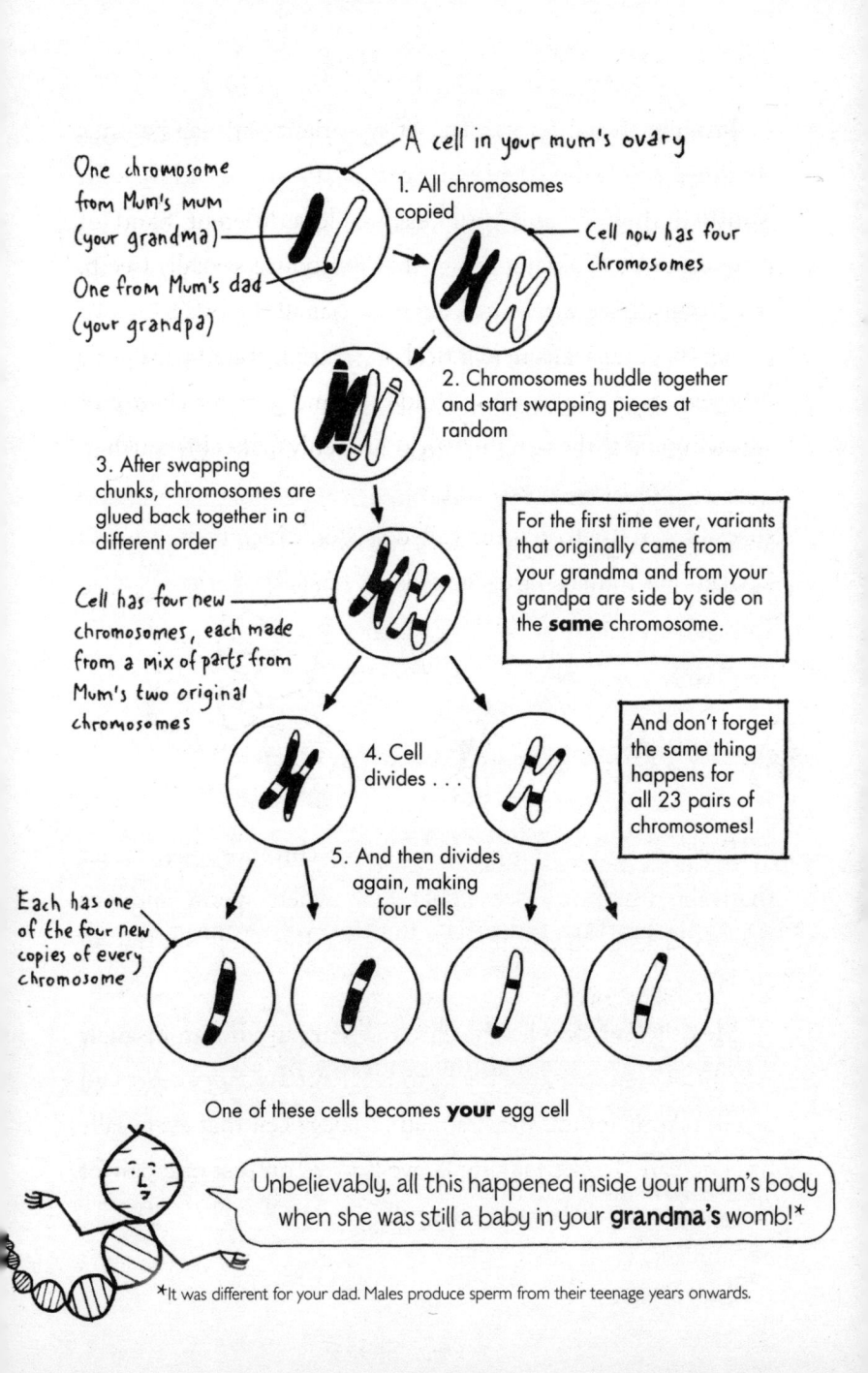

A cell in your mum's ovary

One chromosome from Mum's mum (your grandma)

One from Mum's dad (your grandpa)

1. All chromosomes copied

Cell now has four chromosomes

2. Chromosomes huddle together and start swapping pieces at random

3. After swapping chunks, chromosomes are glued back together in a different order

For the first time ever, variants that originally came from your grandma and from your grandpa are side by side on the **same** chromosome.

Cell has four new chromosomes, each made from a mix of parts from Mum's two original chromosomes

4. Cell divides . . .

And don't forget the same thing happens for all 23 pairs of chromosomes!

5. And then divides again, making four cells

Each has one of the four new copies of every chromosome

One of these cells becomes **your** egg cell

Unbelievably, all this happened inside your mum's body when she was still a baby in your **grandma's** womb!*

*It was different for your dad. Males produce sperm from their teenage years onwards.

Something similar happened when your dad's cells divided to make the sperm that fertilized your egg cell. When that sperm and that egg came together, they each delivered a random mix of gene variants that originally came from all four of your grandparents.

Two parents' genes can get shuffled up into trillions of different combinations during meiosis and fertilization. Which means every child is, quite literally, one in 70 trillion. Even so, two siblings from the same biological parents share around half of their inherited genetic variants. That's why they're usually a bit similar and a bit different. But because meiosis deals out gene variants randomly:

Some siblings share less DNA – so they're a bit more like unrelated strangers

And others share more DNA – so are more like identical twins

As for brothers and sisters, there's a whole chromosome's difference – an extra 1.8% of the entire genome! That's because of the sex chromosomes (see p.67–8):

Females have two X chromosomes (one from each parent):

Males have an X and a Y: X from Mum Y from Dad

The Y chromosome containing the SRY gene is only there to kickstart the development of male bodies (see pp. 64 & 125).

A whole chromosome, just to do that?!

If you're an identical twin, you and your sibling will have grown from the same fertilized egg, so you were dealt the same hand of gene variants.*

THE VARIOUS VARIANTS THAT MAKE US VERY VARIABLE

So what do your gene variants actually do?

Surprisingly, because most variants crop up in junk DNA (see pp. 72-75), most of them probably make no difference at all. On the other hand, when new mutations affect a gene or its regulatory sequence, it can be a very different story.

Let's imagine this sentence is a gene:

THE FAT CAT IS COSY.

And a single mutation is a typo that changes a letter at random. It can change the meaning...

a little bit: **THE FA**B** CAT IS COSY.**
Or a lot: **THE FAT **R**AT IS COSY.**
Or not much at all: **THE FAT CAT IS CO**Z**Y.**
Or make the gene totally mean*less*:

THE FAT CQ**AT IS COSY.**

---

* Your cells will have picked up a few new mutations since they split, so your genomes won't be 100% identical today.

If that sentence really was one of your body's crucial genes, and a new mutation ruined its meaning, it could cause a lot of trouble. That's why cells work so hard to spot mutations and put them right, before they can do any damage. Cells usually do a pretty good job of it, so, luckily, gene variants that cause serious damage are quite rare.

Some do slip through the cracks, though. If we look at a particular variant of Gene's gene, we can see what a big problem even very small DNA mutations can make. When a single A in a particular crucial place is replaced by a T, it plays havoc with the blood's oxygen-carrying haemoglobin (see p. 51), causing a nasty illness called sickle cell disease.

Wow, swapping one tiny letter out of thousands can cause a disease?!

Yes it can. Here's how:

1. Changing one DNA letter changes one amino acid in a protein chain.

2. Gene's protein folds into a slightly different shape.

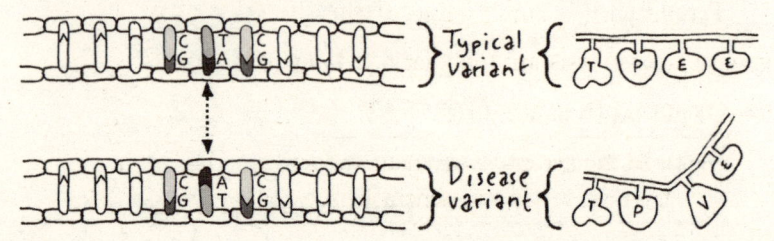

} Typical variant {

} Disease variant {

3. Misshaped haemoglobin proteins make long, sticky chains.

4. Protein chains build up inside red blood cells, making them shrivelled and moon-shaped.

5. Red blood cells clump together and can't carry enough oxygen.

6. Clumps of cells can block veins, causing all sorts of horrible symptoms: e.g. agonizing pain, swollen hands and feet, extreme exhaustion, delayed growth and an increased risk of heart attacks and strokes.

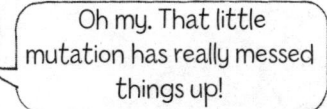

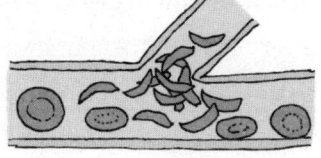

Oh my. That little mutation has really messed things up!

Sickle cell disease is no fun for anyone. But if people inherit just one copy of the sickle cell variant, they don't get ill, because the other 'typical' variant that makes haemoglobin does its job properly.

Two parents, both with one copy of each variant

One child inherits both = gets ill

One child inherits two 'typical' variants = no disease

Third child inherits one of each = no disease

People with a single copy of the disease variant are also resistant to malaria, a dangerous disease spread by mosquitoes.

Hmm. So, like the green pea gene variant, the disease can skip generations.

WHEN MUTATIONS MAKE LIFE BETTER

Sometimes new mutations crop up that don't seem to have a downside at all. Imagine Gene picked up a mutation that made haemoglobin even better at transporting oxygen. If your blood cells contained that mutation, you might be able to run just a bit further or work a bit harder than people who didn't have it, without ever getting tired.

Sounds all right to me.

Helpful mutations, like the one that could improve Gene's design, don't break things, they create things. If they help living things survive and reproduce, they build up over generations, eventually forming totally new genes and causing whole species to change and develop in new and unexpected ways. They make *evolution* happen.*

So, all the amazingly varied creatures that live, breathe, squirm, grow and sprout on this planet today are basically a constantly changing build-up of happy accidents – random mutations that cropped up and just happened to make their cells and bodies work better.

If it wasn't for mutations, none of us would be here at all. So

* To find out more look out for *Explodapedia: Evolution*.

be thankful for them, particularly that variable 1–2% of your genome that makes you, **you**. And remember that everyone else has their own unique set of variants too. Which means that every human being on the planet is basically the same, but also unquestionably different.

CHAPTER 7
The History of You
How Genes Let Us Look Back in Time

It's 11th July 2021, and the English and Italian football teams are battling it out in the final of the European Championships. After 120 minutes, it's still one all. The match will be settled by a nerve-shredding penalty shoot-out.

Five players from each team take turns to step forward, hoping to blast the ball into the back of the net and win the trophy. The crowd holds its breath; the pressure on penalty shooters is truly immense.

Three of the five Italians score. England net their first two kicks, then the next three go astray. Italy's heroes are crowned champions of Europe! The heartbroken English slump to the ground.

It just so happened that the three England players who

missed were Black. A small number of England supporters thought this meant it was OK to hurl a torrent of hateful online *racist* abuse at them.

Sadly, this sort of awful behaviour is nothing new. The abuse aimed at the Black footballers has roots in the Atlantic slave trade of the 16th to 19th centuries. At the time, many Europeans and Americans thought that, because of their differences, it was perfectly acceptable to enslave millions of Africans and strip them of all freedom. Eventually, the trade was outlawed, but racism didn't go away. And, since the early 20th century when, the study of genes first took off, some people have tried to use genetics to back up their racist prejudices.

In the 1930s and '40s, Adolf Hitler, leader of the German Nazi party, took this to its extreme. He claimed that the original inhabitants of Germany were a genetically superior 'master *race*' called Aryans, who were tall, blond-haired and blue-eyed. Without a shred of real evidence, Hitler decided that their genes made them healthier and cleverer than everyone else too.

Err, wasn't Hitler short, dark-haired and always ill?

Yup! Somehow that didn't stop him believing that all other races had inferior genes. And, for Hitler, that meant they had to be controlled, or in the case of Jewish people in particular, wiped out completely.

In 1945, the Nazis eventually lost the Second World War, but racism certainly wasn't defeated. That's why, even in the 2020s, Black sports people all over the world still suffer racist abuse. And each year millions of people, are born into a world of inequality, just because of the colour of their skin or where their ancestors happen to have come from.

Today, scientists can **prove** that genes can **never** be used to justify racism.

If This Is a Race, We're All in it Together

Many racists seem to believe that the way someone looks reveals a lot about what that person is like. Thanks to genetics, we know they're plain wrong. Take your skin colour, for example. It's certainly influenced by particular gene variants. And some of these DNA sequences occur more often in certain parts of the world. But those variants only tell you about one specific thing: how your distant relatives dealt with the sun, way back in the mists of time. It was never about how you deserve to be treated.

Darker skin contains more melanin – a brown-coloured substance that protects skin cells from the sun's harmful UV rays. Basically, people whose ancestors lived closer to the equator tend to have gene variants that increase melanin levels,

Darker skin = more protection from sun but less vitamin D production

Fairer skin = less protection from sun but more vitamin D production

for protection from the sun.

Having a lot of melanin in the skin isn't so crucial for people who live in cooler places. In fact, it can be a problem, because melanin reduces the production of vitamin D, a vitamin that our bodies can only make when sun shines on our skin. Without enough vitamin D, bones don't grow properly and people get sick. Scientists think that's why, thousands of years ago, gene variants that made skin paler became more common the further people lived from the equator, north or south.

In fact, looking beyond skin colour, it's impossible to predict much, if anything, about **anyone**, based on what they look like or where they're from. Wherever you go in the world you'll meet people who vary in pretty much every way – in how they look, think, feel and act. And there are very good genetic reasons for that. When scientists compare the genome sequences of two people chosen at random from the **same** so-called 'race', they see just as many genetic differences as they do when they compare the genomes of people from **different** 'races'.

Wingers need fast legs

Goalies tend to be tall and have BIG hands

All footballers need stamina and good spatial awareness

So, in biology, race is meaningless. Whatever we look like, we're all basically the **same** and we're all wonderfully **different**.

Meet Your Cousins, All Eight Billion of Them

Rather than using skin colour or other visible features to lump people together into different groups, scientists can use DNA to ask a better question: how closely related are we to one another? If the genome sequences of any two random people are 98–99% identical (see p. 79–80), then we must all share ancestors from the not-too-distant past.

Geneticists can use the variable 1–2% to make more detailed comparisons. The closer two people are to having 100% identical DNA, the more closely related they must be, which basically means they shared close relatives more recently.

If you've got a biological brother or a sister, you shared relatives (i.e. your two parents) just **one** generation ago. On average, half of your DNA variants will be the same.

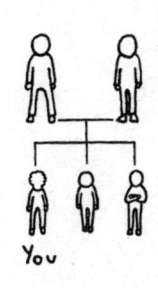

A first cousin, e.g. your mum's brother's daughter, shared relatives with you (i.e. two out of your four grandparents) two generations back. Around one-eighth of your variants will match up perfectly.

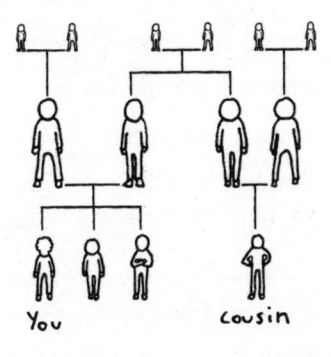

The further back you have to go to find a shared relative, or *common ancestor*, the less DNA, on average, two people have in common.

By matching chunks of DNA, scientists have been able to trace family trees back through time. It's led to some truly mind-boggling findings:

The Bayeux Tapestry is an embroidered cloth that tells the story of William's victory

It is 9 a.m. on 14th October 1066 on the south coast of England. Harold II is King of England and Duke William has just sailed across from Normandy (now part of France). By the time dusk falls, William will have **conquered** the English, earning him his title, the Conqueror, and poor Harold will have caught an arrow in the eye and died.

If your family is originally from Europe, how does it feel to learn that you are directly descended from the victorious King William himself? It's true, you really are.

Then again, the defeated King Harold is one of your distant relatives too. As is every single knight on the battlefield (who survived long enough to have children). When geneticists trace the family histories of different people from **any** part of Europe back in time for 1,000 years, they see that all the different family trees start to overlap. In other words, genes show us that everyone who was living in Europe 1,000 years ago – and who left any *descendants* – is a distant relative of **everyone** with any

European ancestors who's still alive **today**.

Things get even stranger when geneticists look further into the past.

Now we're in ancient Egypt, and it's 1450 BCE. Pharaoh Hatshepsut is ordering those hard-working labourers to finish building her mighty temple.

> I'm building myself a temple.

> If **she's** building it, I'm the Queen of Egypt!

Wherever you come from in the world, according to some geneticists, you can count this high-achieving female pharaoh as one of your direct ancestors.

But don't start getting snooty, because everyone else is related to Hatshepsut too! And anyway, you're just as closely (or distantly?) related to all those long-suffering labourers. If you look back 3–4,000 years, each of our personal family trees contains many millions of branches, which means we each have more ancestors than there were people alive on the whole planet at that time.

Exactly. We're all cousins. We all belong to the same sprawling, unruly and – occasionally – happy family.

Meet Some Long-Lost Relatives

And if all that boggled your mind, hold on to your hats, because we're about to use DNA to travel even further back in time and meet some even more distant relatives. You wouldn't be the person you are today if it wasn't for particular genes or gene variants each of these relatives developed.

800,000 years ago Here's Uncle Ant. Hairier than your other uncles and with terrible table manners, he wasn't even a *Homo sapiens* like you. Ant was a different kind of human – *Homo antecessor*.

Need to invent ... hairbrush!

Thanks to a brand-new variant of a gene called FOXP2, he learned to speak. You've got the same version of FOXP2 in your genome today – it's a transcription factor (see p. 58–60) that switches 'on' genes we need to master speech and language.

13 million years ago Whizzing a few million years further back, here's Nyan, your great-great-great (700,000 times over) grandma.

Hoot, hoot!

Long tail

Even hairier than Uncle Ant

Don't expect much conversation: some scientists think *Nyanzapithecus alesi* is the ancestor you share with orang-utans, chimpanzees and gorillas, so she probably communicated like they do today. Surprisingly, Nyan had basically the same set of 20,000 or so protein-making genes that you have. But your bodies are different because they use those same genes in very different ways.

370 million years ago Let's take a massive leap back and meet Auntie Tiki. Tiktaalik was one of the very first fish to drag itself out of the sea and start living on dry land.

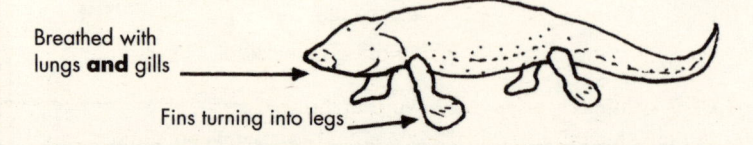

Breathed with lungs **and** gills

Fins turning into legs

Her front **fins** became front **legs** thanks to a new variant that switched 'on' a transcription factor called HOX11. Genes very similar to her Hox11 gene helped make your arms too.

550 million years ago The further back we go, the harder it is to spot the family resemblances. So take a long, hard look at this little slug-like fellow. He's Grandpa Urb, and if it wasn't for a new gene called PAX6 that evolved around the time urbilaterian evolved, you wouldn't be able to look at anything at all.

One of the world's first eyes

PAX6 **still** takes charge of building eyes in all kinds of animals, from fruit flies, to octopuses, to us.

2,000 million years ago Now we're way back in the depths of time, and you might think you've got absolutely nothing in common with Cousin Mito. They're just one cell big, and you've got trillions. But if Mito hadn't developed tiny internal structures called *mitochondria*, there's no way you could have got so big.

Mitochondria provide cell with energy

Mitochondria still power all your cells today. Without them, and the genes they contain, all living things would still be tiny, simple and single-celled. Thanks to Cousin Mito, you're related to every plant, fungus and animal that's ever existed.

4,000 million years ago We're at the very start of life on Earth now. Spare a thought for this little cell, because it's the only living thing that never had any parents. It's called Luca – which stands for Last Universal Common Ancestor – and it's our planet's very first (successful) living cell. Luca discovered how to reproduce, and that's the only reason any of the creatures on this planet (including us) are here now.

Some of Luca's genes are still working inside your cells today, including the ones that build ribosomes (see pp. 47–50).

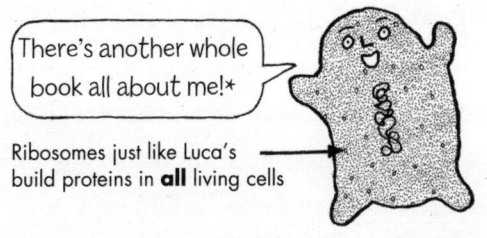

There's another whole book all about me!*

Ribosomes just like Luca's build proteins in **all** living cells

All cells, from the tiniest bacteria to the tallest trees, have relied on those same ribosome-making genes ever since. They all originally got them from Luca. Which means, without a shred of doubt, that all things living on Earth are related.

Wow!

*Explodapedia: The Cell.

CHAPTER 8
Sunshine and Showers
How Gene Forecasts Predict Our Future

Let's travel a couple of decades into the future and listen in on a conversation in a private clinic in a city somewhere near you.

Mr and Mrs Picky are in the process of **choosing** their new baby, and Dr Gene is talking them through the options. Each of the babies she describes will inherit a different combination of Mr and Mrs Picky's genes, and Dr Gene has predicted exactly how those genes will make each child turn out.

This one's a cracker! Tall. Brown eyes, like Mrs P, Mr P's winning smile. He'll grow up with a with a sunny view of life.

Hmmm. We were hoping for a girl who's good at maths.

Well, this embryo will have Mum's gift for numbers and Dad's green eyes, but there's a risk of obesity.

Sounds like science fiction? Well, this conversation is based on a procedure that actually happens in some countries today.

Pre-implantation genetic diagnosis (or PGD for short) is only used for strict medical reasons – at the moment. If one or both parents have a gene variant that causes a serious genetic illness, usually only some of their children will inherit it. PGD can give doctors a way to pick out the embryos that **don't** have the problem gene.

Here's how it works:

1. Eggs are taken from the woman's body and fertilized by the man's sperm in a laboratory. This is called *in vitro fertilization* (*IVF*) and thousands of babies are made this way every year. The next steps are more unusual.

Sperm injected into egg cell

2. Over the next five to six days, the fertilized eggs grow in the lab until they're small ball-shaped embryos (blastocysts, see pp. 62–63). By random chance, some of these will contain the disease gene and some will not.

Blastocyst

3. A small number of cells are snipped from each embryo, without harming it, and their DNA is extracted and used for testing.

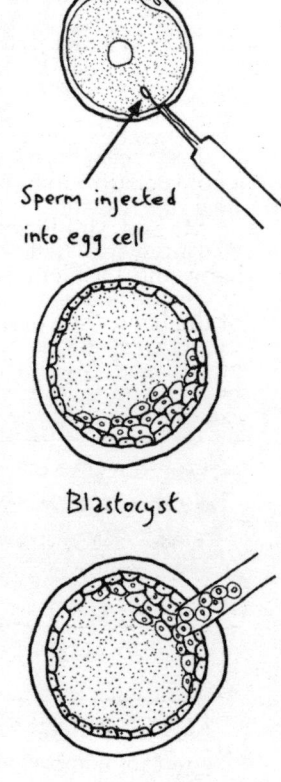

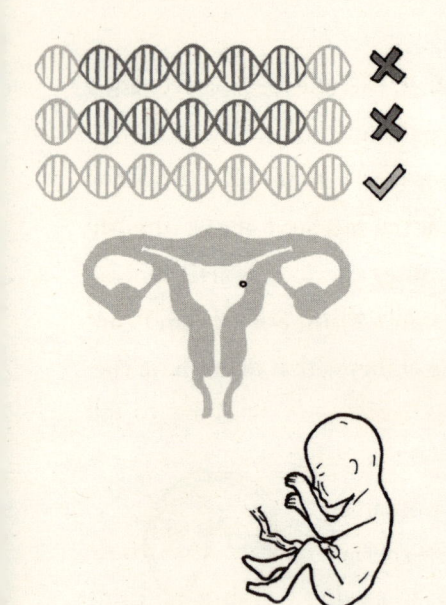

4. Scientists analyse the genes of each embryo, looking for the ones that have NOT inherited the disease gene.

5. An embryo that passes this gene test is injected into the mother's womb.*

6. All being well, the embryo implants itself and develops into a healthy baby, free of the genetic disease.

Every year PGD saves thousands of families from a great deal of suffering.

But, if they had the option, would some parents be tempted to choose features that affect more than just their baby's health? Genetic inheritance is a lottery, so PGD might allow them to beat the odds.

> For just £1 million, I can identify the embryo that will grow into the most beautiful and intelligent child two parents' genes could ever make.

There's a lot about this that sounds wrong – including the high price. What

---

*The embryos that aren't chosen for implantation are either kept alive, but frozen – to use for future pregnancies – or allowed to die (which some people believe is morally wrong).

if only rich people could afford it? Would they perfect their children's genes and leave everyone else behind?

It's a possibility. But first we've got to ask: can gene sequences really predict what kind of human being a tiny ball of cells will become?

The answer to this question really matters, since more and more people are having their genes sequenced today.

• 'Spit-kits' promise to use DNA from your saliva to tell you where your ancestors came from, or what health risks your genes contain.

• Some countries are planning to sequence the whole genome of every newborn baby, to predict health conditions they might suffer from as they grow older.

• Whenever you drink from a cup or bottle, you leave minute traces of your DNA on the rim. Sensitive new tests can use those traces to analyse someone's genes, without them even knowing!

DNA gets sequenced for all sorts reasons, but what secrets can our genes actually reveal?

When Single Genes Have a Lot to Say

Sometimes just one individual gene variant has a big enough effect to alter the workings of an entire body. For example, someone who inherits two copies of the sickle cell disease gene variant (see p. 86–87) will almost certainly suffer from the illness at some point in their lives.

> Do you have to keep bringing up my one imperfection?

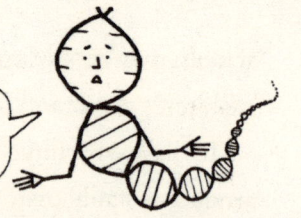

Genome sequencing has helped scientists find hundreds of other single-gene variants that cause a whole range of inherited illnesses and health conditions. Thankfully, most of these variants are rare.

> Ahem! That's no consolation for the people who inherit them!

True. But just knowing about these gene variants can really help people understand where their illnesses come from. It also means doctors and nurses can provide the best care, and scientists can start developing new treatments.

But when it comes to using genes to predict how someone will look and act, single-gene variants are spectacularly useless.

Mr and Mrs Picky would probably never say:

> We'd like a baby with dry, flaky earwax, who hates Brussels sprouts and sneezes in the sun.

> And her pee must smell weird after she eats asparagus!

Health aside, these are the sorts of things Dr Gene can

actually predict by looking one by one at the gene variants of embryos!

To have any hope of picking the embryos most likely to produce a fabulously good-looking, amazingly intelligent or impressively athletic child, she'd have to look at LOTS and LOTS of gene variants all at once.

Complex Characteristics have Complex Causes

When it comes to eye colour, Dr Gene can't really make any promises. It **is** mainly controlled by the genes you inherit. But a 2021 study found a grand total of **61** different genetic variants that seem to influence the variety of shades and patterns of our eyes.

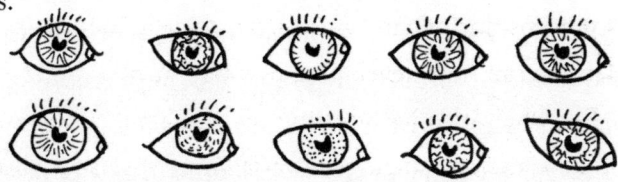

Scientists are still trying to figure out how all these variants work together.

Then there's height ... An incredible **3,000** different gene variants seem to influence this, according to one enormous study.

On their own, most of these variants have very small effects, e.g. by making certain bones grow a tiny bit longer, or a tiny bit shorter. But minuscule nudges add up. Think of it as a kind of sum, with different variants 'adding' and 'subtracting' fractions of millimetres, to explain why some people end up tall and others small.

My jeans are too short!

Short More 'short' variants than 'tall' variants = short

Medium Same number of 'tall' and 'short' variants = average height

Tall More 'tall' variants than 'short' variants = tall

Those eye colour and height statistics come from investigations called Genome Wide Association Studies (GWAS). Since 2005, hundreds of different GWAS studies have searched through the genomes of huge groups of people, looking for gene variants that influence:

• Our appearance (e.g. hair colour, skin tone or nose shape).

• Our bodily health (e.g. the chances of getting asthma or having a heart attack).

• Our mental health (e.g. the likelihood of suffering from serious depression or anxiety).

• Our personalities (e.g. whether we're outgoing, optimistic, etc.).

• Our behaviour (e.g. how likely we are to break the law, gamble or eat healthy food).

• And much, much more.

The studies all come to the same basic conclusion: the way we look, think, feel and act is definitely shaped by our genes, but individual gene variants don't usually have a big effect. Most of the features that make you, **you** are influenced by thousands of different gene variants, which each have small and unpredictable effects.

What's more, genes aren't the only things that shape us. Outside influences have a massive impact too (more on this in the next chapter). For example whichever genes they inherit, children won't grow tall if they don't get enough to eat.

> So predicting **exactly** how an unborn baby will turn out is impossible, right?

Yup, as things stand, it really can't be done. But geneticists are working on it. In the last few years they've developed ways to add up the effects of all the different gene variants that influence a particular characteristic. These are called 'polygenic scores' ('poly' just means 'many', and 'genic' means 'genes') and they can give an idea of how likely our genes are to push our brains or bodies to work in a particular way.

Today, in the 2020s, these predictions aren't usually very accurate. Using them is a bit like forecasting the weather for the same day **next year**; so you **might** get it roughly right, but a detailed prediction will no doubt be wrong. That's a problem for Dr Gene, because her baby reports rely on polygenic scores.

> But I work in the future, remember? Polygenic scores are much better now.

Well, they certainly **might** get better. GWAS studies are getting bigger and geneticists keep finding more powerful ways to crunch all the data.

So what if DNA sequencing actually **did** start to reveal more of the secrets hidden inside our genes? It could raise some tricky issues.

Let's imagine a future government makes it compulsory for everyone to have their entire genome sequenced, then uses the sequences to make personalized gene forecasts. How would you react if you were confronted with those predictions?

In hospital

You're here for a check-up and the doctors say:

> Want to know which illnesses you'll get when you're older?

> We could treat you **before** you get sick.

Do you:

A) Accept straight away. Who wouldn't want to know everything and do all they can to have a healthy future?

B) Run a mile. How can they be sure you'll get any of these diseases? Besides, knowing an illness might affect you will worry you sick.

C) Meet the doctors halfway. You only want to hear about **some** of the health risks. Unless there's a safe and easy treatment, you don't want to know. What's the point of finding out you're likely to die from an incurable disease?

AT SCHOOL

It's your first day at secondary school. Your new teachers have already analysed your gene report card and come up with a plan.

> We can see your brain finds numbers tricky, so we'll give you extra maths lessons.

> And you clearly have trouble focusing – you could be disruptive. A teaching assistant will sit with you in every lesson.

Do you:

A) Get upset. How dare they label you disruptive before you've even set foot in their classroom? You've never caused problems before: just look at your old teachers' reports!

B) Say 'Fair enough.' Maths is your weak point and your attention can wander, so a bit of extra support will do you good in the long run.

C) It's true you hate maths, but you love words, so suggest they help you focus on English instead. Besides, getting distracted is your superpower: it's why you're full of great ideas.

AT A POLICE STATION

These police officers think polygenic scores can help them find criminals before they've committed any crimes, and now they've hauled you in.

> Your genetic makeup puts you at high risk of committing financial fraud.

> You're nicked.

> Don't worry, you won't go to prison. We'll just keep a close eye on you and teach you how to live with your genetic characteristics.

Do you:

A) Trust them. You've got nothing to hide, so where's the harm in being watched? And maybe their training really will make you more trustworthy?

B) Get cross and argue back. You haven't done anything wrong so far and, whatever your genes say, it's your actions that count. C) Call a lawyer and threaten to sue. The police can't know you'll commit a crime in the future. How can they punish you because of the genes you inherited?

Outlook: Stormy Times Are Coming

If gene-based predictions don't improve, but people use them anyway, they could cause a lot of harm: patients could get the wrong medical care, students might get the wrong kind of teaching; and innocent people could end up in trouble with the law.

And even if they do get better, some people will benefit – by staying fit and healthy, say – while others will feel discriminated against because they inherited the 'wrong' genes.

Gene forecasts will never be perfect – our genomes and our lives are just too complicated for that. But as they're used more and more in the years to come, we'd better get ready for some stormy debates.

> When it comes to us genes, you humans sure have a **lot** to think about.

CHAPTER 9
DNA Is Not Destiny
How Our Lives Control Our Genes

In 1940, two identical twin baby boys were put up for adoption at just three weeks old. They joined different families, who, by coincidence, both called their sons Jim. For the next 39 years, the 'Jim Twins' grew up separately, in Ohio, USA, not knowing they had a twin brother just a few miles away.

When they finally got together in 1979, it must have felt a bit like they were meeting their doubles. As well as looking very similar, they both:

- Drove the same kind of car, in the same colour: blue
- Named their sons James Allan (although one spelled it James Alan)
- Had pet dogs called Toy

- Got headaches when stressed

- Bit their nails

- Had done well in maths and woodwork at school, but flunked spelling

- Got married twice: first to a woman called Linda, then to a Betty

Linda Betty

Betty Linda

What was the explanation for all these uncanny similarities? They couldn't all be pure coincidences; DNA must have had quite a lot to do with them. Since Jim and Jim were identical twins, they inherited exactly the same set of genes.

> Wait a minute... how can a gene choose a car? What even is a car?

Right, Gene, the idea that DNA might control our actions so specifically does sound a bit spooky. If genes were in charge of every tiny decision we made, would we all be just pre-programmed robots?

Luckily, that's not how genes work. Because genes lead the process of building our brains and bodies, they have a big influence on the things we do and think. They can certainly nudge us to behave in certain ways or to prefer certain things, but they can't control every tiny aspect of our lives. That would be impossible.

And far too much work for us!

If genes were in charge of everything, identical twins really would be absolutely identical. And they're not. Twins share the same genes, but they're definitely individual people:

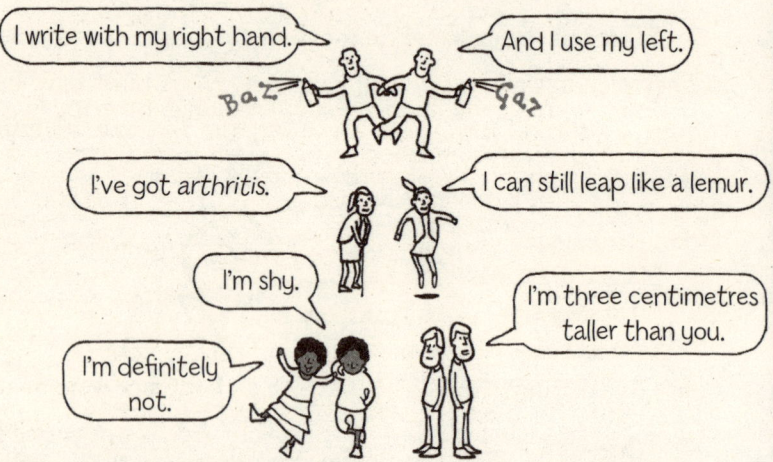

I write with my right hand.

And I use my left.

I've got arthritis.

I can still leap like a lemur.

I'm shy.

I'm definitely not.

I'm three centimetres taller than you.

The two Jims' amazing similarities were recorded by a scientific study that compared lots of pairs of twins. The Jims were the most remarkable set of twins in the study, but they had lots of differences too. For example, they chose different hairstyles, worked in different jobs and, soon after they reunited, one of them got divorced and married his third wife, but the other did not.

Differences between identical twins obviously can't come from the genes, but there are two main ways they do happen:

1. **Random chance** plays a part in the complicated business

of building a human – like the exact way a nerve cell connects with other nerve cells:

Before birth, one identical twin might just happen to have easier access to nutrients and oxygen from the mother's blood, so they'll be born slightly larger than their sibling. Small differences at the start of life can grow into much bigger differences later on.

Take a 'selfie', and you can see the effect random events have on growing bodies. The two sides of your face were made by exactly the same set of genes, but your face is not perfectly symmetrical:

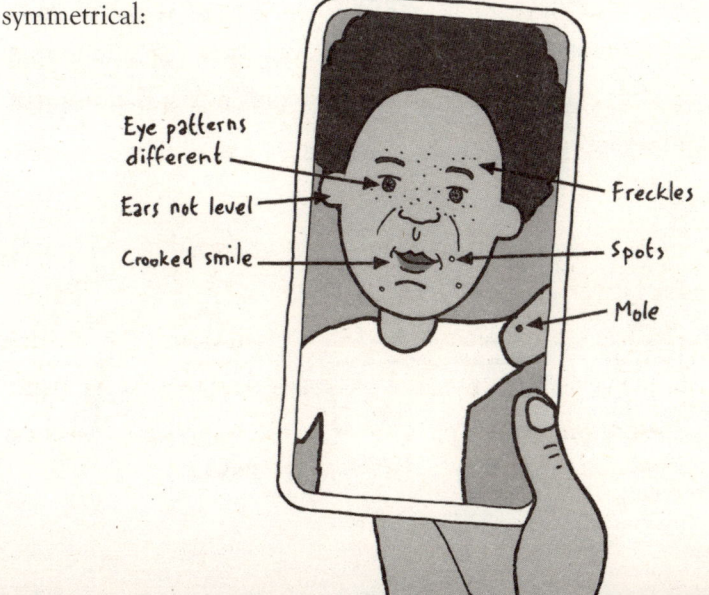

2. **Life experiences** also explain many of the differences between twins. Suppose one set of twins inherits genes that give them the potential to become champion sprinters. If one twin has an accident and breaks their leg as a toddler, they might never be able to run very fast.

In fact, genes are constantly reacting to what's happening in the world around them – scientists call this the influence of the **environment**. It does far more than make identical twins into different people; it affects all of us, in every way possible.

Genes React to the World

What happens when you spend a whole day in the sun? Does your skin tan, freckle, darken, burn or not change much at all? Your genes have a big influence on your skin tone, but so does where you live, the clothes you wear, and applying a dollop of sun cream. In fact, some people deliberately change their skin with fake tan, whitening treatments, or tattoos. So skin tone is never only controlled by our genes, or only by the environment those genes live in.

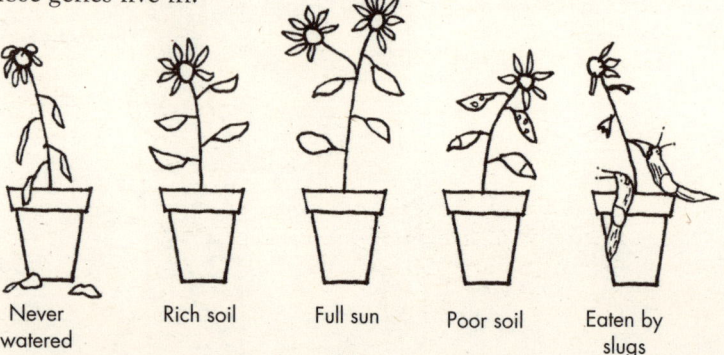

Never watered | Rich soil | Full sun | Poor soil | Eaten by slugs

The same goes for almost every aspect of our existence, including the way we think and act. We are who we are because of genes **and** environment – what some people call 'nature' and 'nurture'. It's always a mixture of both, never one or the other. Apart from rare new mutations that occasionally crop up (see pp. 78-9), genes don't change at all over the course of our lives, but our environments definitely do. While genes make the body, the body has to be able to react when circumstances change. Often, that means changing which genes are used and when.

And those changes can be spectacular, as some recent studies of other animals have revealed.

If you happen to belong to a certain species of *cichlid* fish living in a lake in East Africa, your group will be ruled by one dominant male. He lives like a fishy emperor: he's faster, flashier and fiercer than everyone else. But if the king fish disappears – perhaps on the end of a fisherman's hook – suddenly there's a vacancy at the top. This is the number-two male's chance to shine.

Before

Drab grey skin
Bit scrawny
Nervous
Feeds on leftover scraps

Doesn't mate with females

What a loser!

Several hours later he's a different fish

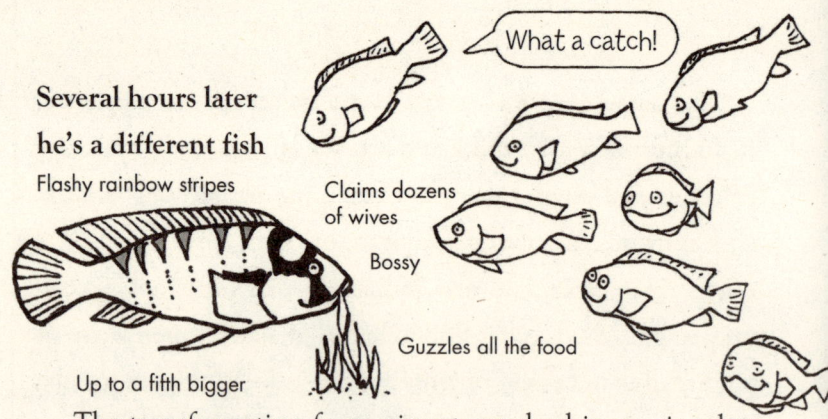

Flashy rainbow stripes

Claims dozens of wives

Bossy

Guzzles all the food

Up to a fifth bigger

What a catch!

The transformation from wimp to warlord is amazing, but all that's really changed is his view of the world. His DNA is just the same, but his new circumstances have triggered hundreds of his genes to turn 'on' and 'off', making him a completely different fish.

How Genes Get Bossed About

For a long time, scientists were baffled by the way changes in the environment could affect the way genes worked. Now they know it's got a lot to do with *epigenetics*. 'Epi' means 'over and above', so epigenetic processes affect our cells, and therefore us, by having an influence on top of our genes. Very often, this involves *epigenetic marks*. These are little chemical notices that get pinned onto genes or regulatory sequences (see pp. 58-9), telling cells how and when to use each piece of genetic information.

When the different cells in your body – in your tongue, teeth, tonsils, toes, etc. – were first being made, epigenetic marks were at the heart of the action. Cells are usually told to differentiate by signalling molecules and transcription factors (see pp. 58-61). As well as flipping genes 'on' and 'off', they can attach new epigenetic marks, making genes stay 'on' or 'off'. That way, cells can remember commands they've received, even after the original instruction is long gone.

Some of the marks on the genes of a skin cell in a developing baby might say:

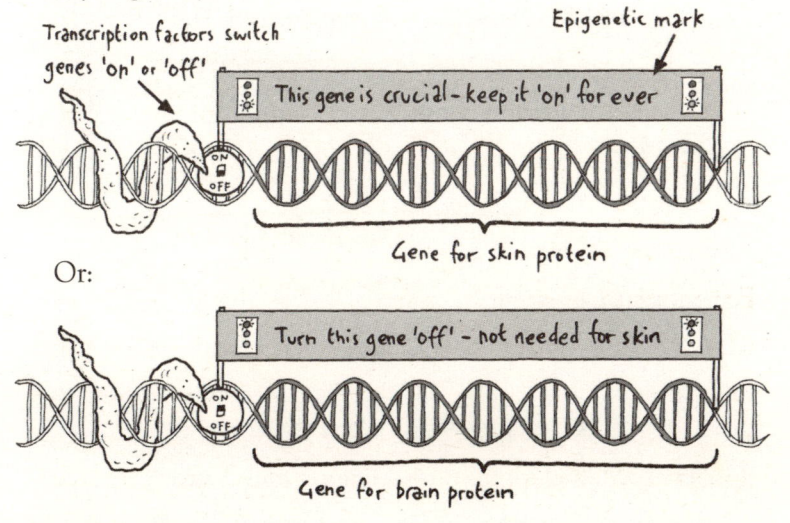

Transcription factors switch genes 'on' or 'off'

Epigenetic mark

This gene is crucial - keep it 'on' for ever

Gene for skin protein

Or:

Turn this gene 'off' - not needed for skin

Gene for brain protein

But epigenetic marks are always busy – even when we're fully grown. Cells are constantly sensing what's going on around them – in other cells, in the blood, or in the world outside – and reacting. Often, that involves adding or removing epigenetic marks, to flip different sets of genetic switches. It means your cells can adapt to – and learn from – changes in their environment. So some of the epigenetic marks in your skin cells **today** might say:

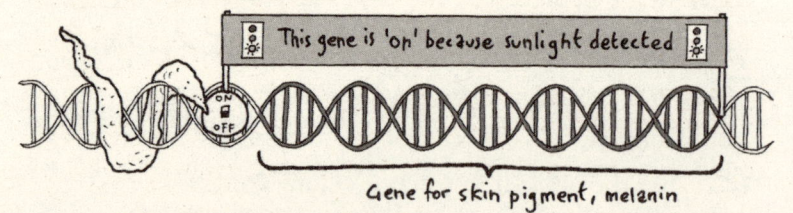

> This gene is 'on' because sunlight detected
>
> Gene for skin pigment, melanin

This gene has reacted to a change in the environment, now it will remember that change.

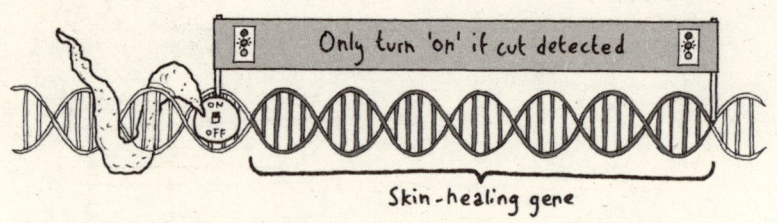

> Only turn 'on' if cut detected
>
> Skin-healing gene

This gene is poised for activation. Under the right conditions, signalling molecules and transcription factors will swoop in and turn it 'on', until the wound is healed and it's turned 'off' again.

Can You Be Whoever You Want to Be?

Some people, including some scientists and doctors, interpret epigenetics as meaning everyone can take the genes they are born with and become the best possible version of themselves. We've just got to make the right choices.

> Study hard and you too can win a Nobel Prize.

> Exercise every day and you can be as strong as me.

> Eat this superfood diet and you'll never get ill.

> Anyone can sing like me if they practise every day.

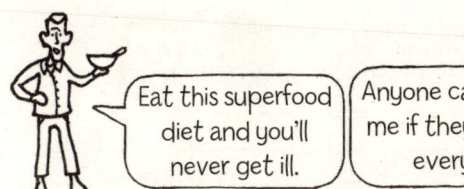

Others approach it differently. Because epigenetics means our bodies remember the past, they say we're always going to suffer as a result of bad things that happened ages ago.

Here's one example of how that could happen.

It's exam day, so you're feeling stressed.

Brain triggers body to make stress *hormones* (signalling molecules) that course through your blood

Stress hormones make your heart pound, your breathing speed up and your mind race

Luckily, these changes don't last long. But if stressful situations don't end – imagine you got badly bullied every day for months – the stress hormones never go away. They can cause longer-lasting, more damaging changes. There's some evidence they can cause epigenetic changes in brain cells, which lead to mental health problems, including anxiety and depression.

Huh? So am I depressed today, because of the bullies who made junior school hell?

Some scientists even think epigenetic 'memories' can occasionally cling onto genes and get passed down from one generation to the next.

So I might be anxious because my dad got injured in a war...?

Experiments have shown that traumatic experiences suffered by an adult rat can affect its children, even when the rat parent never meets its pups. Something similar **might** happen to people, but there's still no definite evidence to prove it.

Chill out, dude, there are no cats about!

This isn't all bad news, though. If we hang onto epigenetic memories of our worst times, the good times must affect our genes too. So love, support and positive experiences really can heal the epigenetic scars from our past.

We may not be able to use epigenetics to completely transform our bodies and brains – like those East African fishy kings – and turn ourselves into whoever we want to be, but there's a lot we can change.

Even our gender identity – whether that's male, female or *non-binary* – is partly determined by epigenetics. People of every gender share all but a few dozen of our 20,000 protein-making genes. Building a male or female body and brain is, therefore, mainly about using the **same** genes in **different** ways, via epigenetic processes.

SRY, a gene on the male Y-chromosome (see p. 64 & 85), kickstarts the epigenetic changes that lead to 'maleness', but in the right circumstances, some of those epigenetic switches can be reversed. That's why *transgender* individuals can, with the help of hormones, treatments and sometimes counselling and surgery, successfully transition from one gender to another.

The genes we inherit do shape us in a big way – that's why identical twins, even the ones separated at birth, usually turn out to be so similar. But epigenetics means that the way our genes work is never chiselled in stone. Our experiences and the decisions we make, quite literally, leave their marks on our genes. Because of epigenetics, the people we meet, the things we eat and even the thoughts we have, mean we each take the genes we inherit and use them in our own unique way.

And, thanks to our powerful brains, we can even choose to push back against the influence of our genes.

CHAPTER 10
Messing Around with Genes
The Promise and Peril of Gene Editing

More than 14,000 years ago, some of our Stone Age ancestors got friendly with one of the deadliest predators around: the grey wolf. As the tamest wild wolves came to live in human camps and breed among themselves, their teeth, jaws and claws gradually shrank, and they became much gentler. Over many generations, these ferocious carnivores turned into loyal pooches.

Prehistoric people then set about transforming all sorts of other living things:

Wild boars became placid pigs

Lean mountain mouflon became meek woolly sheep

Chewy grasses became wheat, barley, oats and rice

This is called *selective breeding*, and for most of history, when people bred animals and plants for their own use, they had no idea they were massively altering the genes of living things. But that's exactly what they were up to.

They had to be patient, though – it can take dozens or even hundreds of years to breed living things to suit human needs. And they couldn't be too ambitious – they could only change a wolf by choosing characteristics associated with wolf gene variants. They couldn't mix in genes from other kinds of living thing:

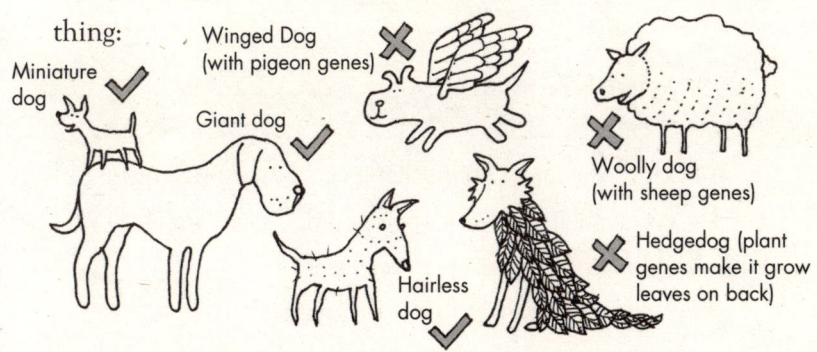

Miniature dog ✓

Winged Dog (with pigeon genes) ✗

Giant dog ✓

Hairless dog ✓

Woolly dog (with sheep genes) ✗

Hedgedog (plant genes make it grow leaves on back) ✗

But, in the 1970s, biologists really did work out how to cut genes out of one living thing and splice them directly into the chromosomes of a completely unrelated creature. They called this *genetic engineering* and, amazingly, the transplanted gene often seemed to work just fine. It proved that genes work the same way in all living things. Some genetically engineered organisms have saved millions of lives.

People with diabetes have trouble controlling their blood sugar levels, which can lead to serious health problems. Their bodies either can't produce a protein called *insulin*, or their cells don't respond to it properly, so often the best treatment is injections of extra insulin. Since the 1980s, most of that life-saving insulin has been made by **bacteria** cells that contain the **human** gene for making insulin.

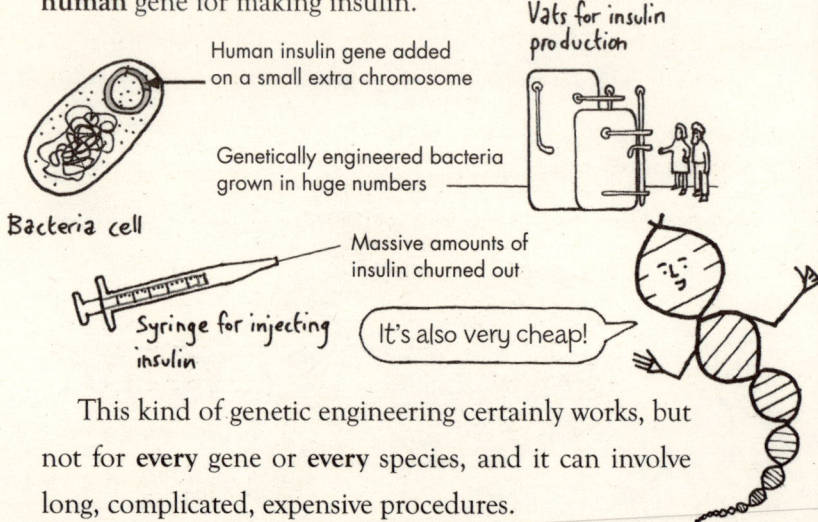

Vats for insulin production

Human insulin gene added on a small extra chromosome

Genetically engineered bacteria grown in huge numbers

Bacteria cell

Massive amounts of insulin churned out

Syringe for injecting insulin

It's also very cheap!

This kind of genetic engineering certainly works, but not for **every** gene or **every** species, and it can involve long, complicated, expensive procedures.

Super-CRISPR to the Rescue!

However, in 2012, scientists Jennifer Doudna and Emmanuelle Charpentier made a scientific breakthrough that changed everything. Almost overnight, genetic engineering became easier, cheaper, more accurate, reliable and flexible.

Biologists often give their new discoveries complicated names that only they can understand, but this one took that habit to a whole new level. Doudna and Charpentier's breakthrough was based on things called **C**lustered **R**egularly **I**nterspaced **S**hort **P**alindromic **R**epeats.

Got that? Good. Let's just call their revolutionary new technique *CRISPR* (say 'crisper') from now on. The key to CRISPR's success is its ability to cut DNA very precisely. It has two parts:

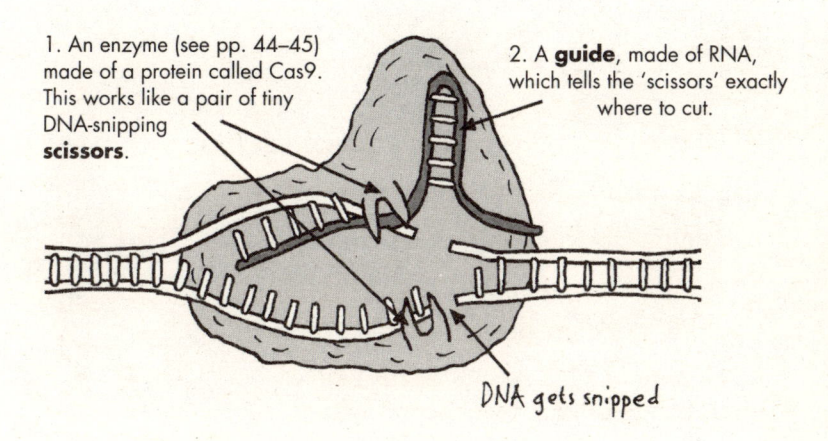

1. An enzyme (see pp. 44–45) made of a protein called Cas9. This works like a pair of tiny DNA-snipping **scissors**.

2. A **guide**, made of RNA, which tells the 'scissors' exactly where to cut.

DNA gets snipped

In 2020, Doudna and Charpentier won a Nobel Prize for their CRISPR invention, but in truth, it wasn't **their** discovery at all.

What we call CRISPR was actually invented billions of years earlier by tiny microbes. To this day, bacteria are constantly being attacked by viruses; and their CRISPR system works as a kind of immune defence. Here's how:

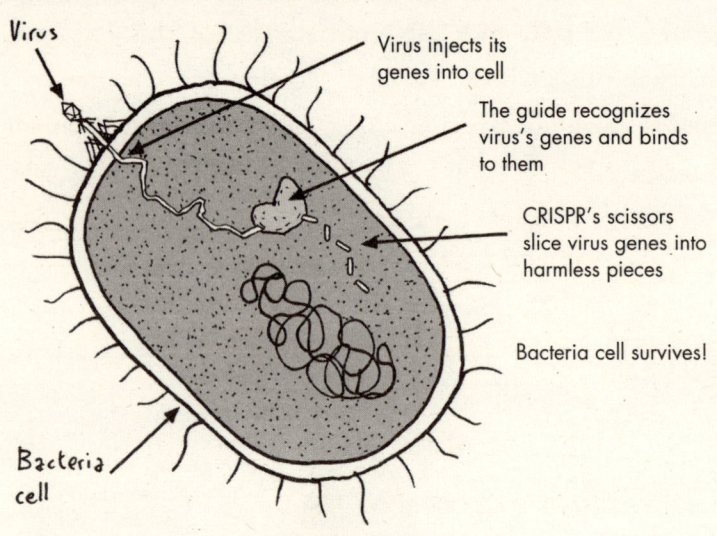

- Virus
- Virus injects its genes into cell
- The guide recognizes virus's genes and binds to them
- CRISPR's scissors slice virus genes into harmless pieces
- Bacteria cell survives!
- Bacteria cell

Doudna and Charpentier's genius idea was to turn CRISPR enzymes into tiny, programmable DNA-altering robots.

By changing the guide, they could make CRISPR work on practically ANY piece of DNA code in ANY species, at ANY time.

CRISPR actually makes altering DNA instructions a bit like editing a text document on your computer – hence the name *gene editing*. Imagine this sentence was a piece of DNA:

THE DOG CANNOT FLY

Scientists can:

> **'Cut'** the DNA, so it says:
>
> **THE DOG CAN~~NOT~~ FLY**
>
> Any number of DNA letters, from one to many millions, can be deleted

'Copy and paste' the DNA, to make it say:

THE DOG with pigeon genes CAN FLY

> A new piece of DNA from any other species can be inserted into cuts made by CRISPR

Make smaller **'edits'** to the DNA:

THE HOG CANNOT FLY

> When single DNA letters are changed, it is sometimes called prime editing

Give genes more **'emphasis'** (so they produce more mRNA):

THE DOG CANNOT FLY!

Or make them less obvious, by turning their activity down:*

the dog cannot fly

---

*Scientists keep changing and improving the CRISPR system to alter DNA in more precise ways. Now they can even change DNA without cutting it, e.g. by altering epigenetic marks (see pp. 120–122).

How Gene Editing will Change our World

As well as making it possible to tweak the genes of almost any species, CRISPR made creating completely new kinds of living thing – sometimes called *synthetic biology* – much easier.

Nobody has made a flying dog – yet. Luckily, most geneticists have been using their tools for more useful projects.

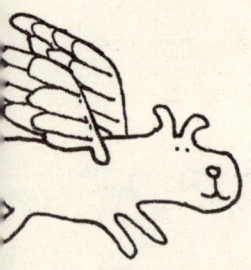

The following are just a few of the exciting gene-based ideas that are already being developed. They could improve our lives, and even the whole planet, but they'll probably throw up tricky questions too ...

Genes to stop disease

Mosquitos spread all kinds of nasty diseases, including malaria, dengue fever and Zika virus. Every year they make about 700 million people ill, killing around a million of us.

This is a massive problem for humans, and scientists have answered it by creating gene-edited mosquitoes that could spread their genes through entire wild mosquito populations, stopping them breeding and so stopping the illnesses!

Ending malaria would be world-changing, but could using gene-edited mosquitoes this way cause serious problems?

> Yup. Especially for all the birds, bats, fish and frogs that feed on mosquitoes!

GENES TO END WORLD HUNGER

Hundreds of millions of people around the world go hungry every day, but the global population keeps growing. Farmers need to produce more food, more easily, while creating less pollution and harming less wildlife. That's why scientists are devising gene-edited crops that:

- **Use genes from bacteria to make their own natural nitrogen fertilizer** Farmers could use less fertilizer, so it wouldn't run off their fields, poisoning rivers, lakes and seas.

- **Produce toxic substances that kill insect pests** That would mean bigger harvests, and no need to spray crops with nasty insecticides.

- **Contain extra vitamins, like vitamin A, to make food more nutritious** Around 500,000 kids go blind each year because they don't get enough vitamin A.

- **Grow in poor soils with barely any water** These would be revolutionary, especially in places where the climate crisis is already causing terrible droughts.

But it won't all be easy or risk-free.

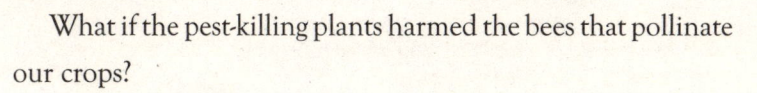

What if the pest-killing plants harmed the bees that pollinate our crops?

And if these new crops were developed by big private companies, would profit come before saving the world?

GENES TO MAKE STUFF MORE SUSTAINABLY

Synthetic biologists can turn living cells into tiny but incredibly efficient factories that churn out all kinds of astonishing new products, with hardly any waste. These actual inventions could be available everywhere, just a few years from now:

Trainers made from super-strong spider silk instead of artificial fibres. The silk is produced by yeast cells that contain spider genes.

Aircraft running on carbon-neutral jet fuel, made by gene-edited algae, just using sunlight, water and air.

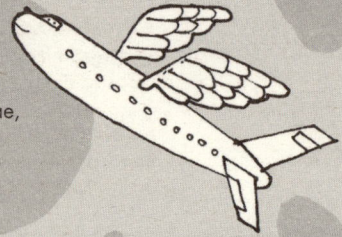

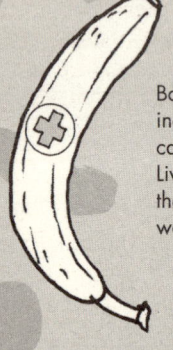

Bananas containing edible vaccines. Medicines, including vaccines for diseases like COVID-19, can be made by gene-edited cells and plants. Living cells make complex chemicals far more easily than human chemists can, saving energy, reducing waste and creating better medicines.

Parts of a touchscreen and electronic circuits on a smartphone made by gene-edited microbes, including new features like bendable screens.
 Since biological parts are much easier to recycle, this means less destructive mining of rare minerals.

Scientists haven't found any serious downsides to these inventions yet. But they do need to work out how to make these products in serious quantities and more cheaply.

Gene editing has the potential to transform far more than just the world's farms, factories and pharmacies . . .

CRISPR Can Edit YOUR Genes Too

In 2019, an American woman called Victoria Gray became one of the first people in the world to have her genes edited. She had sickle cell disease (see pp. 86–87) and her doctors used CRISPR to treat her.

• They took the blood-making stem cells from Gray's bone marrow.

• They edited the cells' genes to switch 'on' a working version of the gene that makes oxygen-carrying haemoglobin.

• The 'fixed' stem cells were injected back into Gray's body, and they've been making red blood cells with working haemoglobin ever since.

It's wonderful. It's the change I've been waiting on my whole life.

Some doctors dare to believe we're at the beginning of a medical revolution. Gene editing **could** one day be used to 'correct' practically any troublesome variant, to treat or prevent all kinds of health conditions, from cancer, heart disease and dementia, to infections caused by bacteria and viruses.

A massive amount of research and safety testing has to happen before gene editing becomes an everyday part of your trip to the doctor's, though. While we wait for that to happen, let's take a peek into the future and meet a doctor with even bigger plans for CRISPR . . .

Enhanced Humans?

Remember Dr Gene from Chapter 8, and her promise of perfect babies? Another decade has now gone by and she's launched a brand-new service, which she hopes Mr and Mrs Choosy will go for.

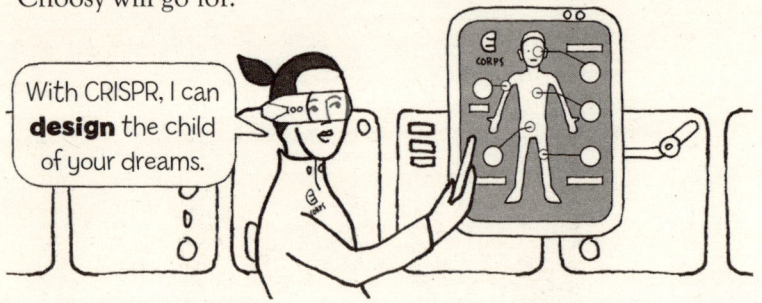

> With CRISPR, I can **design** the child of your dreams.

What she's suggesting would be called genetic enhancement and it goes way beyond making sure babies grow up fit and healthy.

Here are some of the amazing options you can choose from:
$ € ¥ £
Genius-level intelligence
Muscles of a pro swimmer
Resistance to all known viruses
Film star beauty
Self-confidence of a top politician
Guaranteed 130-year-plus healthy lifespan
It sounds unbelievable!
Exactly. That's why I brought my biologist sister along.
And I say, **don't do it**! There's loads that could go wrong.

Sure, Dr Gene can edit any genes she wants to **try** to create an exceptional child. But unless scientists of the near future learn a **lot** more about our genomes, it's extremely risky – for three main reasons.

1. **Nobody knows which genes to edit** That's especially true for complicated characteristics, like intelligence and personality (let alone something as personal as beauty!). To have any chance of making a baby that's a genuine genius, Dr Gene might have to edit hundreds of different variants at the same time.

> Even if we could do that, we wouldn't know how making so many changes at once would affect the baby.

2. **Unintended consequences** During the 1990s, scientists made genetically engineered tomatoes that looked perfect and didn't rot. But they hardly tasted of anything! The genes that affected shelf life also affected flavour. That's normal: most genes do lots of different jobs.

> Editing brain genes to make a child more intelligent could accidentally cause something like depression, memory problems or even worse conditions.

3. **CRISPR isn't perfect** Occasionally, and for no obvious reason, CRISPR cuts DNA in the wrong places. These mistakes could be devastating.

They could wreck a crucial gene like me!

I'm sure I can make it work. We'll check for slip-ups!

Call me old-fashioned, but it just sounds too risky...

Don't Mess with the Germline (for now)

There's another big problem with Dr Gene's 'designer baby' plans. To make sure her 'improved' genes were in **every** cell of a child's body, she wouldn't just be choosing tiny embryos, she'd be altering their genomes at the tiny embryo stage.

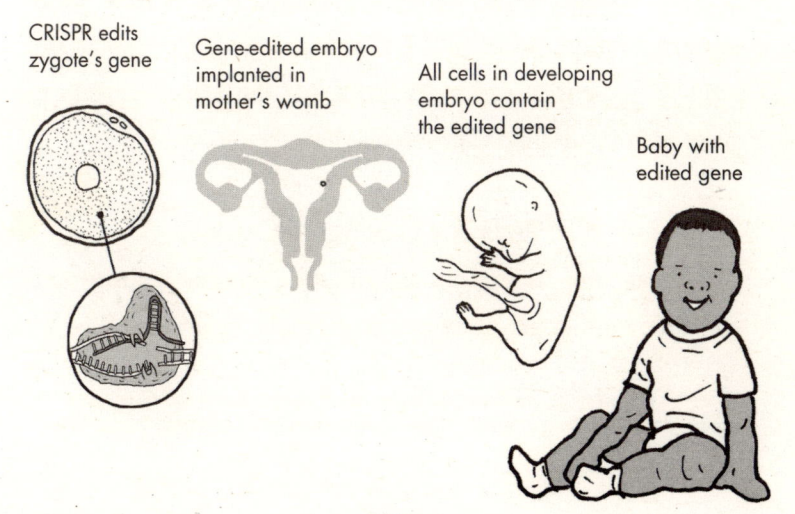

CRISPR edits zygote's gene

Gene-edited embryo implanted in mother's womb

All cells in developing embryo contain the edited gene

Baby with edited gene

This is called *germline gene editing*, and it wouldn't just affect that growing embryo. Its children and its children's children would also inherit the edited genes.

> So could it also remove genetic illnesses like sickle cell disease from entire families, once and for all?

> It certainly could, but any mistakes would affect all of them... for good.

Today's scientists have proved that gene editing tiny embryos works, but most of them agree that allowing them to grow into babies is still just too risky. Germline gene editing is currently banned in almost every country.*

That could change, though, particularly if a new, more accurate version of CRISPR is developed, and if – and it's still a big 'if' – scientists can really prove that the edits they want to make won't cause more problems than they solve.

Get Ready for Even Bigger Changes

Each year, the tools and techniques for gene editing and synthetic biology get more powerful, more accurate and easier

---

*A scientist who edited the genomes of twin babies born in China in 2018 landed three years in prison following his dangerous experiment. Nobody quite knows what happened to the germline gene-edited babies.

to get hold of. Scientists have even started **writing** completely new genes, and even whole genomes, from scratch. That means they can design proteins, cells and entire organisms that have never existed in nature before.

We can't know what the future holds. One day, gene editing babies might seem perfectly normal. And, as we're about to see, that could change the human race completely and for ever.

There's No Such Thing as Normal

It's my 100th birthday and I'm fit as a fiddle!

Haemoglobin genes redesigned to carry four times as much oxygen. Muscles keep working at max power for longer.

Genes edited to reverse ageing. Scientists are trying to do this today, e.g. by copying genetic 'tricks' from age-defying animals – like flatworms and jellyfish.

We're at the Olympic Games 2080, and the 100m race is just starting. By now the world has taken Dr Gene's gene enhancement ideas and literally run away with them, so these sprinters have a few genetic advantages!

If gene editing really was risk-free, and worked exactly as planned, would you want it, for you or for any children you might have in the future?

I dunno ... it seems so unnatural. Isn't it cheating?

Depends how you look at it. Vaccines and antibiotics are 'unnatural'. And moving to a better school and using the internet to get smarter could be seen as 'cheating'. Is choosing particular genes, or even editing them to improve someone's life, really so different?

Well, people almost certainly **will** be tempted. And that could cause big problems, even if the gene editing itself becomes totally safe.

Perhaps only rich, successful people would be able to afford to do it for themselves and their families. Then their children would become even more . . . rich and successful.

> What would happen to all us 'ordinaries' without any enhancements?

We'd have to hope future governments would make gene editing easy and cheap. That way everyone could iron out their genetic flaws and try to design the children of their dreams.

That sounds fairer. But would it really be a good thing?

> Of course! Every child deserves the chance to live a normal life, without suffering. That's what CRISPR can deliver.

> But how do **you** know what counts as suffering?

> And what the heck do you mean by 'normal'?

Good questions. Because of our genes:

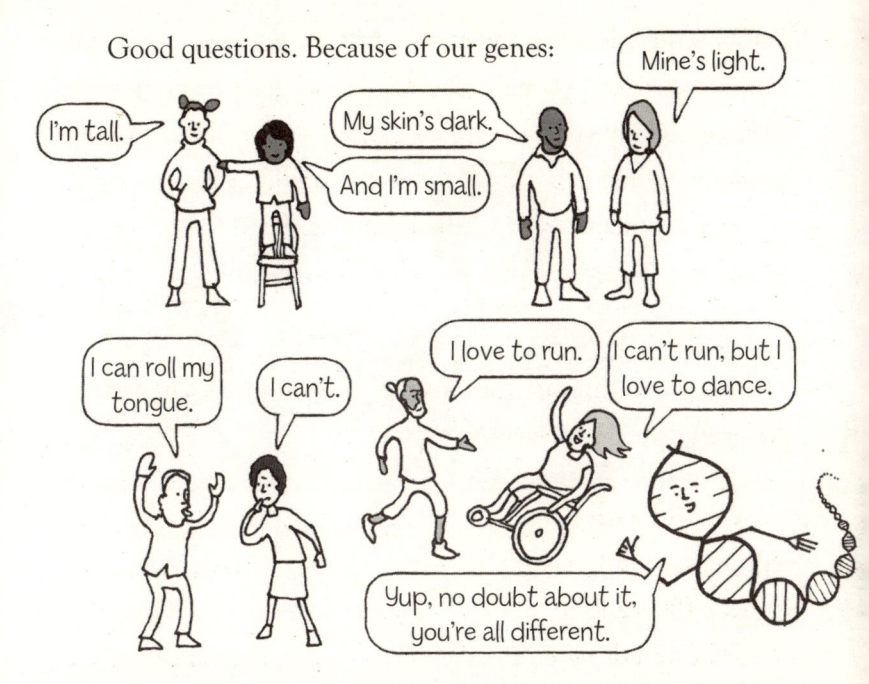

I'm tall.

My skin's dark.

Mine's light.

And I'm small.

I can roll my tongue.

I can't.

I love to run.

I can't run, but I love to dance.

Yup, no doubt about it, you're all different.

No one has, or ever will have, **exactly** the same DNA as you. And by now, you can probably understand how your distinctive genes are constantly shaping **everything** you think, feel and do. So there's no such thing as a 'normal' genome. Or a 'normal' person.

The most creative, life-changing ideas often bloom in the minds of people who see the world in the most different ways. They also pop up when very dissimilar people meet, or when we struggle to overcome the challenges life throws at us.

If gene selection and gene editing really did take off in a big way, they couldn't suddenly be used to make us, or dogs, sprout wings. But lots of much subtler alterations could still change our lives dramatically. Would we lose those genetic differences that make us who we are and start to become pretty much the same?

Life would be so boring!

And we might start running out of fresh ideas. The fact is, we need diversity to survive.

Of course, it **might** never happen. Germline gene editing could end up being limited so it's only used to treat inherited illnesses that are incurable. More ambitious plans to tweak people's genes might fail.

So we don't need to panic. But we do need to think about these possible futures, before they barge into our lives and change everything for ever.

And don't forget, there's still so much you don't know about us genes!

Yup. Even now, biologists don't all agree on what a gene actually **is**! And our chromosomes still contain huge tracts of code – in the junk DNA and beyond – that have scarcely been explored. What secrets might they be hiding?

Until we've got a much better grasp of how our genomes

work, it's best not to fiddle with them **too** much.

If you hear people saying someone isn't 'normal', what they really mean is, because of their differences they don't quite fit their current surroundings. It's usually easier to change those surroundings, i.e. the environment, than it is to try and change the person – or their genes.

- Discovered you've got a food allergy? Don't eat that food.
- Short-sighted? Get glasses or contact lenses.
- Maths too hard? Get help from teachers or online.

The obstacles we face – on our own, in our families, or in our wider communities – don't all have such easy solutions.

> But the fact is ... if you change your world, you change the way your genes **work**.

Precisely. So instead of rushing to 'fix' everyone's genes, maybe we should try harder to 'fix' the world. What if we could make it into a place where everyone has a chance to succeed, whichever genes they inherit?

A place where we can truly celebrate the unbelievable fact that we're all the same, and we're all different ...

> And there's no such thing as 'normal'.

TIMELINE: HOW GENES HAVE CHANGED LIFE ON EARTH FOR EVER

Living creatures on this timeline, including some of our (very) distant relatives, are shown at the estimated time they first appeared on Earth.

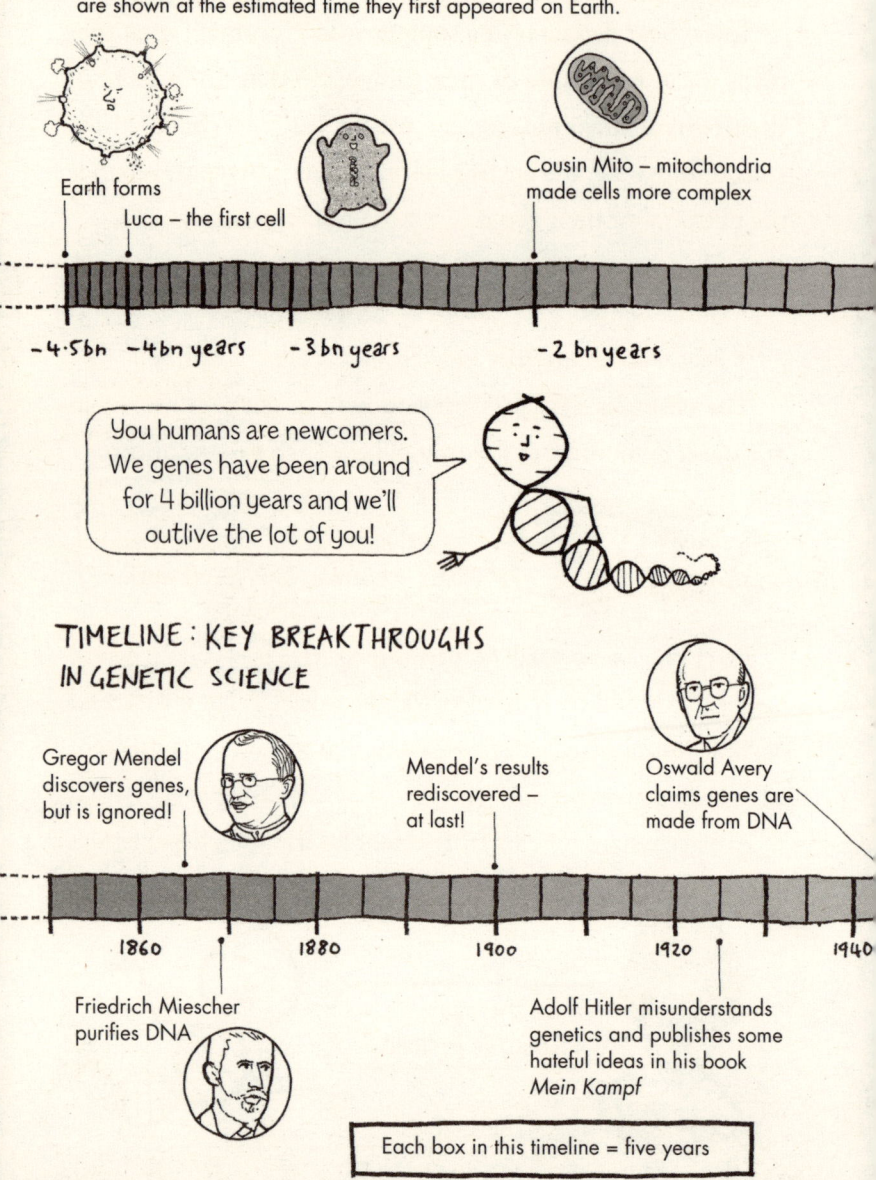

Earth forms

Luca – the first cell

Cousin Mito – mitochondria made cells more complex

-4.5bn   -4bn years   -3bn years   -2 bn years

You humans are newcomers. We genes have been around for 4 billion years and we'll outlive the lot of you!

TIMELINE: KEY BREAKTHROUGHS IN GENETIC SCIENCE

Gregor Mendel discovers genes, but is ignored!

Mendel's results rediscovered – at last!

Oswald Avery claims genes are made from DNA

1860   1880   1900   1920   1940

Friedrich Miescher purifies DNA

Adolf Hitler misunderstands genetics and publishes some hateful ideas in his book *Mein Kampf*

Each box in this timeline = five years

Each box in this timeline = 100 million years

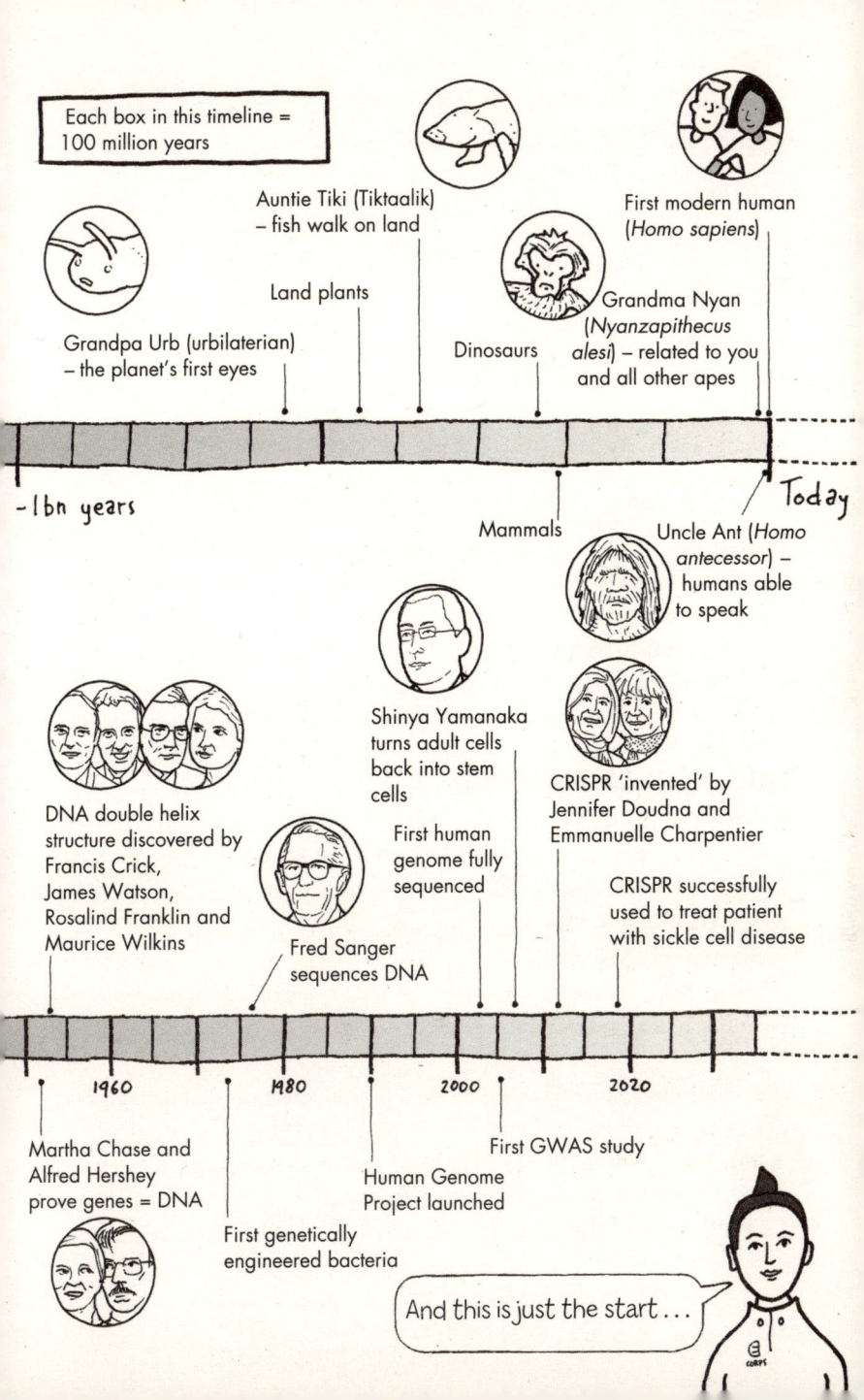

Grandpa Urb (urbilateralian) – the planet's first eyes

Land plants

Auntie Tiki (Tiktaalik) – fish walk on land

Dinosaurs

Grandma Nyan (*Nyanzapithecus alesi*) – related to you and all other apes

First modern human (*Homo sapiens*)

−1 bn years

Mammals

Uncle Ant (*Homo antecessor*) – humans able to speak

Today

DNA double helix structure discovered by Francis Crick, James Watson, Rosalind Franklin and Maurice Wilkins

Fred Sanger sequences DNA

Shinya Yamanaka turns adult cells back into stem cells

First human genome fully sequenced

CRISPR 'invented' by Jennifer Doudna and Emmanuelle Charpentier

CRISPR successfully used to treat patient with sickle cell disease

1960 1980 2000 2020

Martha Chase and Alfred Hershey prove genes = DNA

First genetically engineered bacteria

Human Genome Project launched

First GWAS study

And this is just the start…

Glossary

Words that are in italics have their own entries in this glossary.

amino acids small *molecules* that link together to make *proteins*

ancestor a member of your family from whom you are directly descended. Your parents, grandparents, great grandparents, etc. are your ancestors, but your uncles, aunts, cousins, etc. are not

atoms extremely small particles that bond together to build up all living and non-living things

bacteria tiny, single-celled *organisms*. One of the main kinds of *microbe*

base the part of a *nucleotide* in an *RNA* or *DNA molecule* that makes up a single 'letter' of *genetic* information

base pairing the precise way two *nucleotides* with matching *bases* link together to join the two *strands* of a *DNA molecule*

biological parents the people or living things that provide the sex *cells* from which an individual living thing grows

biological sex whether an *organism* is male, female or other, based on the physical characteristics and reproductive organs they possess

cell the smallest thing that can definitively be called 'alive'. Cells can live on their own as single cells, or together as parts of larger bodies

cell division when single *cells* make more cells by copying their *genes* and then splitting into two

characteristic a feature that belongs to a certain individual or group

chemical bond a powerful force that holds *atoms* and/or *molecules* together

chromosomes long *DNA molecules*, with *proteins* attached, that contain a *cell's genes*

common ancestor the most recent direct relative (see *ancestor*) shared by two different individual living things or *species*

CRISPR a powerful and precise tool used for *gene editing* living *cells*

cytoskeleton a network of long, connected *protein* fibres inside a *cell*. The cytoskeleton gives a cell its shape, protects it, moves things around inside it and also allows some cells to move themselves around

descendant someone who is directly related to a particular *ancestor*

differentiate/differentiation when a *cell* is changed so that it can do a particular job, e.g. form part of a growing heart

DNA (deoxyribonucleic acid) long, string-like *molecules* that carry information and form a *cell's genes*

DNA sequencing the process of determining the order of the four *nucleotides* in DNA

dominant a dominant *gene variant* overrides the effect a *recessive variant* of the same gene has on a particular *characteristic*, e.g. eye colour

double helix the spiralling, two-stranded structure of *DNA molecules*

ectoderm a layer of *cells* on the outside of an early-stage animal *embryo* that will go on to make brain, nerve and skin cells

embryo a living thing going through its earliest stages of development

endoderm a layer of *cells* on the inside of an early-stage animal *embryo* that will produce throat, gut, lung, liver and pancreas cells

environment the surroundings or conditions a living thing exists in, any of which can potentially influence the way its *genes* work

enzyme a substance in a *cell* that can make, break, change or join together different kinds of *molecule*

epigenetics the scientific study of how the characteristics of *cells* or *organisms* are affected when *genes* are turned 'on' or 'off', without actually changing their DNA code. Often involves epigenetic marks – small chemicals that bind to genes, changing the way they work

evolution the way the inherited *characteristics* of living things change over mulitple generations

fertilize when two *cells* fuse together to make a new *embryo*, e.g. when an egg cell from a female animal joins with a male sperm cell

foetus the unborn offspring of a human or other animal

gender identity whether individuals consider themselves to be male, female or *non-binary*. They may have been assigned a different *biological sex* at birth

gene editing using technology to make precise changes to the *DNA* code of *cells* or living things

gene/genetic each gene contains a specific instruction for how to build (from *protein* or *RNA*) a particular part of a *cell* or body. Genes are made from *DNA* and are passed down from one generation of a living thing to the next

genome the complete set of *genetic* instructions in an *organism*

germline the cells that produce the eggs or sperm that carry genes from one generation to the next

haemoglobin a substance in blood that transports oxygen around the bodies of most vertebrates (animals with backbones)

Homo sapiens the species you belong to. Modern humans

hormones *signalling molecules* that carry messages between the different parts of a living thing's body

hydrogen bond a fairly weak *chemical bond*, based on hydrogen *atoms*, that can either link two *molecules* or join parts of the same molecule

insulin the main *hormone* that controls the amount of glucose (sugar) in your blood

intron part of a *gene* that does not contain information and has to be removed in order to build a working *protein* or *RNA*

IVF (in vitro fertilization) a medical procedure where an egg *cell* is *fertilized* by a sperm cell outside of the body, in a laboratory

meiosis the kind of *cell division* that makes sex cells (e.g. sperm and eggs in animals and pollen and eggs in plants)

membrane a thin, oily protective layer that surrounds a *cell* and also surrounds different structures inside it

mesoderm a middle layer of *cells* in an early-stage animal *embryo* that will go on to produce cells in the muscles, heart, kidney, bladder and reproductive organs

messenger RNA (mRNA) a copy of a particular *gene's* code, made from *RNA* containing the information needed to make a new *protein molecule*

microbe a living thing that is too small to be seen without a microscope

mitochondria structures inside living *cells* where chemical reactions take place that are needed to produce crucial energy-carrying *molecules*

mitosis when one *cell* divides to make two cells, which both contain an identical set of *genes*

molecule two or more *atoms* joined together by *chemical bonds*

mutation a change in a *gene* or *chromosome's DNA* structure, which might be passed down through generations

nanometre one thousand millionth of a metre

non-binary somebody whose *gender identity* isn't male or female

nucleotide the basic building block of nucleic acids (*RNA* or *DNA*). There are four different DNA nucleotides: adenine (A), cytosine (C), guanine (G) and thymine (T). In RNA, uracil (U) replaces thymine

nucleus a *cell's* main control centre, which contains the *genes*

organism a living thing

ovum an egg *cell*

PGD (pre-implantation genetic diagnosis) a technique used to assess an *embryo's genetic* information during the very earliest stages of its development, before it embeds in a mother's womb

protein a large *molecule* that is essential for all living things. Proteins have many functions in *cells*. These include building structures, controlling chemical reactions and sending and receiving messages

race an artificial grouping of people based on: a) where their families are originally believed to have come from and b) perceived similarities in the way they look and/or act. According to most genetic studies, separate human races do not actually exist

racist discriminating against or attacking other people who are assumed to belong to a different *race*, based on the mistaken belief that some races are inferior to others

recessive a *gene variant* whose effect on a particular *characteristic* (e.g. hair colour) can be overruled by a *dominant variant* of the same gene

regulatory sequences parts of a *gene* involved in controlling where and when that gene is switched 'on' or 'off'

reproduce/reproduction to produce new copies of a living *cell*, by *cell division*; or to make a new generation of living things

ribosome a structure found in all living *cells* that turns the instructions contained in *genes* into *molecules* of *protein* that can then work for the cells. Where *translation* happens

RNA (ribonucleic acid) a chemical similar to *DNA*. One of its main jobs is delivering messages from DNA *genes* to the rest of the *cell*

selfish DNA pieces of *DNA* code that make more copies of themselves in order to spread inside an *organism's genome* without benefitting the organism in any way

signalling molecules chemical substances that carry useful information between living *cells* or organs, or from one part of a cell to another

species a specific kind of *organism*. The members of a species have similar *characteristics* and shared relatives

stem cell a general-purpose *cell* that can divide itself to make new cells, which then *differentiate* to do specific jobs

strand a long, stringlike chain of connected *nucleotides* that binds to a matching strand of DNA to form a *double helix*

synthetic biology the science of creating living *cells*, or parts of cells, that do not naturally exist

transcription factors *proteins* that switch *genes* 'on' or 'off', so they start or stop making the RNA needed to make other proteins

transcription the process of making an *mRNA* molecule that contains a copy of the information held in a *gene's DNA*

transfer RNA folded RNA molecules that carry *amino acids* into *ribosomes* during the *translation* of *proteins*

transgender someone whose *gender identity* is different from the one they were assigned at birth

translate/translation the process of using the *genetic* information in an *mRNA molecule* to produce a *protein* molecule

transposable elements a kind of *selfish DNA* that can move itself around inside a living thing's *genome*

variant an alternative version of a *gene* or *chromosome*, created through a permanent change in its DNA structure. Variants can involve any number of DNA *nucleotides*, from one to many millions

viruses a minuscule living particles that can only *reproduce* inside the *cells* of a different living thing. Some can cause diseases

x-ray crystallography a scientific technique for working out how *atoms* join together to form the structure of *proteins* or other large *molecules*

zygote a single *fertilized egg cell*, which has the potential to develop into a complete human or other many-celled *organism*

INDEX

A
amino acids 48, 49, 50-1, 86
ancestors 74, 78-9, 83, 92, 93, 94-101, 105, 126
Avery, Oswald 28, 148

B
babies, development of 54-5, 60-6, 121
bacteria 13, 28, 29-30, 101, 128, 130, 133, 136, 149
base pairing 37-8, 49
bases, DNA 33, 35, 37, 39
biological parents 10, 17-18, 19, 22-3, 67, 81-4, 95
blood, circulation of 52

C
cell division 15, 37-40, 44, 62, 68, 78, 82-3
cell membrane 9
cells 10-11, 101
  changes in 57-8, 77-8, 86-7, 121-2
  differentiation 56-7, 59, 60, 62, 63, 65, 121
  DNA and 45-53
  working of 41-5, 53
characteristics 18-19, 20-3, 127
  predicting children's 12, 102-7
Charpentier, Emmanuelle 129, 130, 149
Chase, Martha 28-30, 149
chromosomes 67-9, 73, 74, 77, 79-80, 82-3, 84-5, 128, 146
cichlid fish 119-20
climate crisis 133
common ancestor 94-95, 101

Crick, Francis 32-4, 149
CRISPR (Clustered Regularly Interspaced Short Palindromic Repeats) 129-32, 135-6, 139, 140, 149
crop plants 127, 133, 138
cytoskeleton 43

D
designer babies 136-9, 140-1, 142-4
differentiation 56, 57-61, 62, 63, 65, 121
disease 86-7, 103-4, 105-6, 108, 110-11, 128, 132, 135-6, 146, 149
diversity 17, 146
DNA (deoxyribonucleic acid)
  in cells 45-53
  in chromosomes 68-9
  copying of 37-40
  discovery of 26-8
  in genes 28-30
  junk 73-6, 78, 85, 146
  life's information 11, 35-7, 76
  mutations 77-81, 86
  structure of 31-4, 149
DNA sequencing 70-1, 92, 94, 105-6, 110
dominant gene variants 22-3
double helix 34, 37, 149
Doudna, Jennifer 129, 130, 149

E
eggs 10, 14, 16, 55, 67, 78, 82, 83, 84, 85, 103
embryos 64, 102, 103-4, 107, 139-40
environment 118-20, 122, 147

enzymes 44-5, 49, 53, 129, 130
epigenetics 120-5, 131
evolution 17, 88, 99-101
eye colour 18, 65, 107, 108

F

family trees 95-8
fertilization 10, 16, 20, 55, 67, 82, 84, 85, 103
food production 13, 133
Franklin, Rosalind 30, 31-3, 149

G

gender identity 64, 125
gene editing 12, 13, 126-41, 142-4, 145
generations 17, 20, 21, 23, 24, 39, 78-9, 88, 95
genetic engineering 12-13, 128, 128-31, 138
genetic enhancement 136-9, 142-4
genetic information 11-12, 27, 35-7, 45-7, 72, 120
Genome Wide Association Studies (GWAS) 108, 110, 149
genomes 67, 70-6, 78-9, 80-1, 82, 84, 85, 93, 94, 105, 106, 108, 110, 138, 141, 145, 146-7, 149
germline gene editing 139-40, 146

H

haemoglobin 36, 40, 51-2, 53, 56, 86-7, 88, 135, 142
height 107-8
Hershey, Alfred 28, 30, 149
Hitler, Adolf 91, 148
Homo antecessor 99, 149
Homo sapiens 99, 149
human body, development of 54-66, 85, 121, 125
human genome 70-2, 149
hydrogen bonds 33, 37, 38

I

in vitro fertilization (IVF) 103-4
inheritance 22-4, 67, 81-5, 87, 103, 104, 106, 107, 109, 113, 115, 140
intelligence 138

J

junk DNA 72-6, 78, 85, 146

L

Last Universal Common Ancestor (Luca) 101, 148
life on Earth 8, 9, 101, 148-9

M

malaria 87, 132
meiosis 82-4
Mendel, Gregor 19-24, 25, 27, 39, 67, 70, 77, 148
mental health 108, 123-4
messenger RNA (mRNA) see RNA
microbes 14, 130, 134

Miescher, Friedrich 25-8, 148
mitochondria 67, 100-1, 148
mitosis 15
molecules
  DNA 8, 31-4, 39, 40, 68
  protein 35, 50-2, 56
    see also signalling molecules
moral issues 104, 110-13, 140
mutations 77-89, 119

N

nature and nurture 119
nerve cells 57, 60, 63, 117
nucleotides (adenine, thymine, cytosine, guanine and uracil) 33, 34, 35, 37, 46, 70
nucleus, cell 9, 26, 47
Nyanzapithecus alesi 99, 149

O

oxygen, transportation of 36, 51, 52, 88

P

parasites 74, 76
plants, reproduction 16, 20-4, 39
pollen 16, 20, 133
polygenic scores 109-10, 112
pre-implantation genetic diagnosis (PGD) 102-5
protein folding 50-1
proteins 26, 27, 35, 44, 45, 46-51, 53, 56, 58, 61, 73, 99, 101, 125

R

race/racism 91-4
random chance 83, 84, 85, 88, 93, 103, 116-17
recessive gene variants 22-3, 87
red blood cells 51, 53, 56, 87, 135
regulatory sequences 58-9, 61, 73, 75, 85, 120
reproduction 14-24, 37, 40, 44, 62, 82-3, 88, 101
ribosomes 47-50, 53, 101
RNA (ribonucleic acid) 46, 47, 56, 61, 73, 129
  guide RNA 129
  messenger RNA (mRNA) 46-7, 49, 58-9, 131
        transfer RNA (tRNA) 46, 47, 48, 49

S

Sanger, Fred 70-1, 149
selective breeding 126-7
selfish DNA 74, 76
sex cells 82; see also sperm, egg & pollen
sex chromosomes 67, 84-5
sex determination 64, 84-5, 125
sexual reproduction 16-17, 20, 22, 82-3
siblings 81, 84-5, 95, 114-15, 117
sickle cell disease 86-7, 105-6, 135, 140, 149
signalling molecules 60, 61, 121, 122, 123
single cell organisms 14-15, 100-1
skin colour 18, 65, 91-4, 108
species, evolution of 88-9
sperm 10, 16, 67, 78, 82, 83, 84, 103
SRY gene 64, 85, 125
stem cells 63, 135, 149
strands, DNA 33, 34, 37-40, 47
synthetic biology 132-4, 140

T

Tiktaalik 100, 149
transcription 47, 58-9
transcription factors 58-9, 61, 62, 64, 99, 100, 121, 122
transfer RNA (tRNA) see RNA
transgender people 125
translation 47-50
transposable elements 74, 78
twins, identical 19, 82, 84, 85, 114-18, 125

V

vaccines 67, 142
vacuoles 47
Virchow, Rudolf 58-9, 62, 64, 149
viruses 15, 17, 43, 67

W

waste disposal 29, 42-3, 137
water 31, 34, 44, 52, 88

Y

Yamanaka, Shinya 127-8, 129, 131, 149

Acknowledgements

Our immense gratitude to editor Helen Greathead. Without her ideas and hard work, this book would be far denser! Huge thanks to designer Alison Gadsby, for bringing everything to life on the page. Anthony Hinton steered the project and chipped in with excellent ideas. Thanks to copy and proof editors Julia Bruce and Jennie Roman for their sharp eyes and shrewd comments, to sensitivity readers Kasey Robinson and Ravyn M. Evermore for notes on Chapters 7 and 9, and to indexer Helen Peters. It's been a pleasure working with the wider DFB team, including Bron, Fraser, Phil, Rosie, Meggie, Jasmine and Rachel, to get this book out into the wider world. Massive thanks to David Fickling for dreaming up this approach to non-fiction, and to Michael Holyoke and Liz Cross for helping turn vision into reality. Finally, warmest thanks to Professor Alison Woollard, of the University of Oxford, for checking facts and allowing us to tap her deep knowledge of genetics.

BM: From one generation to the next, genes can only build on what came before. So, it feels right to acknowledge the scientists and writers whose work I've mutated and recombined into something new and, hopefully, distinctive. They include Steve Jones, Adam Rutherford, Siddhartha Mukherjee, Matthew Cobb, Matt Ridley, Carl Zimmer, Ed Yong and Paul Nurse. Thank you all.

About the Author and Illustrator

Ben Martynoga is a biologist and science writer. After a decade in the lab exploring the insides of brain cells, he swapped his white coat for a pen. Since then he has written about everything from the latest tech innovations to rewilding, running, stress, creativity, microbes and the history of science. He loves talking about science – and why it matters – with children and adults alike at science festivals, in classrooms or anywhere else. His writing appears in the *Guardian*, *New Statesman*, the *i*, the *Financial Times* and beyond. He lives, works, wanders and wonders (often all at once) in the Lake District.

Moose Allain is an artist, illustrator and prolific tweeter who lives and works in South West England. He runs workshops and has published a book and an online guide encouraging children to draw, write and find inspiration when faced with a blank sheet of paper. Always on the lookout for interesting projects, his work has encompassed co-producing the video for the band Elbow's 'Lost Worker Bee' single and designing murals for a beauty salon in Mexico City – he's even been tempted to try his hand at stand-up comedy. His cartoons regularly feature in the UK's *Private Eye* magazine.

In 2020, Ben wrote and Moose illustrated *The Virus*. They are currently working on more books in the *Explodapedia* series.

EXPLODAPEDIA

The Gene is just one piece of a larger world of knowledge. There is plenty more to discover, and *Explodapedia* will be your guide!

Where will your curiosity take you next . . . ?

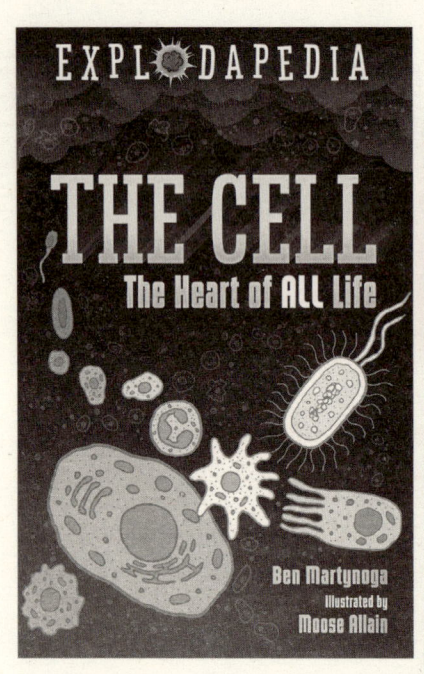

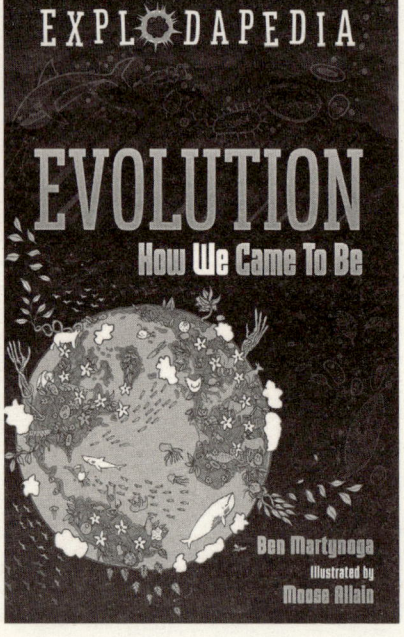